THE
Glory
of God IS
Intelligence

THE Glory of God is Intelligence

Four Lectures on the Role of Intellect in Judaism

Jacob Neusner

University Professor
Professor of Religious Studies
The Ungerleider Distinguished Scholar of Judaic Studies
Brown University

VOLUME THREE
IN THE RELIGIOUS STUDIES MONOGRAPH SERIES

Introduction by
S. Kent Brown

Religious Studies Center
Brigham Young University

For

Robert Goldenberg

Contents

Preface

The invitation to return to Brigham Young University and to present a series of four lectures was particularly welcome to me. For Brigham Young University provides a unique forum for scholars of religions, consisting, as it does, of faculty and students who take seriously the claims of one religion, and who also preserve the commitment to intellect and critical thought which make possible scholarship on all religions. I was glad to accept the invitation of our former student at Brown University, Professor S. Kent Brown, who teaches ancient scriptures at Brigham Young University, further to prepare lectures which might be published as a reasonably coherent statement on a topic of common interest.

For that purpose I present four lectures on a theme of importance to my Mormon hosts and to my topic of specialization, Judaism. Intellectuals of The Church of Jesus Christ of Latter-day Saints, my hosts, face the question of how through the use of their minds in essentially academic and intellectual pursuits they may understand themselves to be servants of God. The thought of Judaism on the centrality of learning — learning in Torah, revelation — in the service of God — seems to me a particularly relevant and appropriate topic. As indicated, it also permits me to draw together some diverse, and now completed, researches of mine, so that I may see how the results of various projects relate to a single problem. For this purpose I draw heavily upon available writings, reorganizing and extensively revising them for the present purpose, which is, in sequence, theological, historical, and literary in focus.

The theme of these lectures, then, is the distinctive conception of Judaism that we serve God through the use of our minds. The mythic expression of that conception, contained in the words *Talmud Torah,* study of divine revelation, of course makes the idea rather particular to Judaism. My effort here is to spell out the theological, historical, and literary traits of the ideal of *Talmud Torah* as the very center and heart of Judaism. I address myself, therefore, not to the generalized philosophical notion that intellect and worship go hand in hand. Rather, I turn to the concrete and specific one that *Talmud Torah* outweighs all other religious and moral obligations, that the central symbol of Judaism is the scroll of the Torah, that the heart of the liturgy of Judaism is the hearing of the Torah read in the synagogue, and that the principal religious action called for by Judaism is to learn Torah.

I propose to explain three things, first, the theological meaning of *Talmud Torah,* second, the point in the history of Judaism that *Talmud Torah* enters the center of Judaic life, and, third, the particular document which, in addition to the Pentateuch, the written Torah received by Moses at Mount Sinai, is deemed by Judaism to constitute Torah, requiring study, interpretation, and concrete exegesis in every aspect of the good life. In so doing, I propose to draw together a number of lines of reflection and research into what I hope is a coherent account of what I conceive to form the heart and soul of Judaism.

I appreciate my hosts' invitation to make these lectures available for publication. While speaking from a written manuscript, rather than an outline, requires considerably greater preparation, the possibility of sharing these papers with a wider audience provides ample compensation. I have tried to produce lectures worthy of both the excellence of their audiences in Provo and the interest and attention of those elsewhere who may read them.

Documentation for these lectures will be found as follows: Lecture One, *Invitation to the Talmud;* Lecture Two, *The Rabbinic Traditions about the Pharisees before 70;* Lecture Three, *Eliezer ben Hyrcanus: The Tradition and the Man* and *A Life of Yohanan ben Zakkai,* and *Development of a Legend: Studies on the Traditions Concerning Yohanan ben Zakkai;* Lecture Four, *A History of the Mishnaic Law of Purities.* XXI, *The Redaction and Formulation of the Order of Purities in Mishnah and Tosefta* and XXII, *The Mishnaic System of Uncleanness: Its Context and History.*

J.N.

Provo, Utah
June 10, 1977
Sivan 22, 5737

Acknowledgments

My colleague, Professor Richard S. Sarason, Brown University, kindly read these lectures at several stages in their formation and offered important criticisms.

I express my thanks for the exceptionally cordial hospitality accorded to my wife and children and to me by our hosts in Provo. My several trips to the West in general, and to Utah in particular, have always been happy experiences, because they provide an encounter with people of unusual human depth and resonance and an opportunity to learn from the spiritual understanding of thoughtful and serious friends. My LDS hosts in Provo opened their hearts to me, expressed their inner convictions and concerns, and opened their minds and hearts to what I had to say as well. Israel speaks to Israel, gentile to gentile, in a perfect confusion of roles: Provo to me is not alien.

The work is dedicated to a former student, now himself settled out West, who as both an educator and a scholar explores important aspects of the ideal of *Talmud Torah* in Judaism.

Introduction

When, on October 5, 1976, at the request of BYU's Forum Committee I wrote to Professor Jacob Neusner to invite him to deliver an address at a Forum Assembly of the student body, neither he nor I could have guessed that our correspondence during the next few months would lead to these four lectures. The overall concept of the lectures came to him, as he typifies such strokes of insight in his first lecture, in a "moment of inexplicable understanding . . . in which all things fall together into a whole, . . . a moment of revelation" as it were. During the first four months of 1977, the correspondence between Dr. Neusner and myself consisted largely of suggestions and counter-suggestions regarding topics and titles not only for the Forum lecture but also for three additional presentations which he had graciously consented to prepare. We were then contemplating four lectures somewhat divergent in focus and content. Then on May 3, Professor Neusner telephoned me to say that, inspired by the phrase "The glory of God is intelligence," which appears as part of the logo on the University's stationery, he had decided to offer a summary of almost a decade of study in four interrelated lectures on Judaism's most distinctive aspect: learning as devotion to God.

In taking up the dictum "The glory of God is intelligence," Professor Neusner has brought into sharp focus the paramount feature of the transcendence of God. The phrase, of course, derives from Mormon scripture: "The glory of God is intelligence, or, in other words, light and truth." (Doctrine and Covenants 93:36.) The holy books of the Latter-day Saints are replete with the notion that intelligence and knowledge constitute essential ingredients in the eternal scheme of man's existence and progression. A few examples will illustrate this point. In the Doctrine and Covenants the idea of salvation is linked directly with the dispelling of ignorance: "It is impossible for a man to be saved in ignorance" (131:5). Further, in section 130 of the same book we read: "Whatever principle of intelligence we attain unto in this life, it will rise with us in the resurrection. And if a person gains more knowledge and intelligence in this life through his diligence and obedience than another, he will have so much the advantage in the world to come." (D&C 130:18-19.) One explicit directive, among others, to acquire intelligence is found in section 88 of the Doctrine and Covenants: "Seek ye out of the best books words of wisdom; seek learning, even by study and also by faith" (88:118). Mormons, then, possess a theology which includes, nay, embraces the concept that the processes of salvation, the steps to sanctification, are profoundly and inseparably connected with the acquisition of knowledge and intelligence, a result being that one is enabled to "comprehend even God." (D&C 88:49.)

Almost at the dawn of the existence of The Church of Jesus Christ of Latter-day Saints stood the School of the Prophets, organized by Joseph Smith in December 1832, as the educational arm of the priesthood. The school was designed to instruct the brethren regarding "things both in heaven and in the earth, and under the earth; things which have been, things which are, things which must shortly come to pass; things which are at home, things which are abroad; the wars and the perplexities of the nations, and the judgments which are on the land; and a knowledge also of countries and of kingdoms." (D&C 88:79.) This concept of learning, even commandment to study, underscores the idea that for Latter-day Saints, too, learning may be thought of as an act of devotion to God, an action which possesses transcendent meaning. This notion as it appears in Judaism forms the major focus of Professor Neusner's Forum address, the first of the four lectures.

The next three lectures report the origin and development of the ideal of Torah-learning in Judaism, the careful study and scrutiny of what God revealed in the law in order that it might be practically applied in the everyday living of Jews. Pivotal in the development of this ideal are the events of A.D. 70, the year that saw the fall of Jerusalem and the destruction of its temple at the hands of the Romans and their general, Titus. More than anything else, these catastrophic events laid on Jews the onus of restructuring their lives in the absence of the temple which was both central to and imparted meaning to life for Israelites. The two groups that survived the fall of Jerusalem and that achieved varied success in giving order to the lives of their adherents after the temple's loss were Christians and Pharisees. It is to the latter that Professor Neusner draws our attention in these lectures.

It has been concluded almost universally by scholars of Judaism of late antiquity that pre-70 Pharisaism had already developed the ideal of a piety manifested in studying Torah, God's law, oral or written. It is this conclusion that Dr. Neusner questions in Lecture Two. There exists no evidence, he observes, for this notion in the sources, which include the New Testament books, the writings of the Jewish historian Josephus, and the Mishnah and Tosefta, both redacted about A.D. 200. In fact, after one lays aside the biases in the sources towards the Pharisees, pro and con, one discovers that Pharisees were determined to follow a course in life that sought to imitate the ritual purity practiced by the priests of the temple. The religious inclinations of the Pharisees, then, were inspired by the centrality of temple worship, as were most Jews, except with more intensity, especially on issues that involved ritual cleanness in eating and tithes on foods. Consequently, the idea that Pharisaic religiosity before 70 was deeply rooted in an intense study and systematic interpretation and application of the law cannot be sustained.

Such a phenomenon appears only in the aftermath of the war

against Rome when, in the wake of the loss of the temple and its sin-offerings and the corresponding ruin of the ideal of the temple's purity being *replicated* in each home in Jerusalem, the Pharisees restructured Jewish life by teaching that ritual offerings of the cult could be *replaced* by acts of loving-kindness, the temple's purity by cleanness in every Jew's workaday life, and, most important, worship of God through sacrificing by study of Torah. This new synthesis, in which stress fell on the study of Torah as the vehicle of devotion and rabbi took the place of priest, became known as Rabbinic Judaism. Tracing this development forms the core of Lecture Three.

In Lecture Four, Dr. Neusner makes plain the remarkable qualities of the Mishnah, that summary of legal commentary on scripture which arose from the synthesizing work of the rabbis and scribes who worked at the small academy at Yavneh during the decades immediately before and after the second disastrous revolt by Jews against Rome led by Simeon bar Kokhba beginning in A.D. 132. What is to be underscored, argues Professor Neusner, is the open-ended, timeless, continually contemporaneous character of the Mishnah which emerges from the warp and woof of its language, its repetitive structure, grammar, and syntax. The recurrent structures of Mishnah's language serve not only to replace the regular and recurring symbolic acts of the now lost ritual of the fallen temple but also to communicate order, meaning, and transcendent value to the incidents of everyday living. In achieving this form of communication through repetitive, holy language, the rabbis broke with the past since they chose not to encapsulate their insights within books which they then attributed to Adam or to Moses, such as done by pseudepigraphists, nor did they cast their ideas into the linguistic patterns of ancient texts, such as done by the sectarians of Qumran. Instead, the language of the Mishnah, each time it was approached, led its readers to fresh perspectives on one's relationship to God. The basic vehicle to these fresh insights is the mind, the seat of intelligence. Such is the nature of the Mishnah.

The illumining contribution made in these lectures towards understanding the development and essential character of Judaism is obvious to any reader. Professor Neusner has won our warm appreciation for accepting the invitation to return to Brigham Young University. And we express our deeply felt thanks to him for making these significant lectures available for publication.

S. KENT BROWN

Provo, Utah
June 10, 1977

1

"The Glory of God Is Intelligence" A Theology of Torah-learning in Judaism

What one person means by the religious, another understands as secular. To us Jews and to you Mormons, food-taboos express an aspect of the religious life. To others they do not. Religious folk may learn from one another—which is our task this day—when we illuminate those religious convictions and concerns which we share. One such trait, shared by the Jewish religion and the religion of The Church of Jesus Christ of Latter-day Saints, is the conviction that religion thrives through the use of the mind and intellect. Skepticism and critical thinking are friends, not enemies, of religion. That is why intellectuals of the Mormon faith will grasp the conviction, expressed in the particular language of Judaism, that *Talmud Torah*—study of divine revelation—outweighs all else, that the human being was made to study Torah, and many other sayings which express the same idea. In this lecture I want to offer a theology of learning in Judaism which may supply a fresh perspective on why learning may be deemed by Mormons to be not merely a useful, secular value, but an act of religion and of sanctification.

Brigham Young University came into being, as you all know,

when, in 1876, Brigham Young, President of The Church of Jesus Christ of Latter-day Saints, gave Karl Maeser the following commission: "You are to go to Provo, Brother Maeser. I want you to organize and conduct an academy to be established in the name of the Church—a Church School." And he added: "I want you to remember that you ought not to teach even the alphabet or the multiplication tables without the Spirit of God." No informed Jew can find alien or strange such an ideal, an ideal expressed in the motto of this university, "The Glory of God Is Intelligence." For the most distinctive and paramount trait of Judaism as it has been known for the past two thousand years is the conviction that the primary mode of the service of God (not the sole mode, but the paramount one) is the study of Torah. Torah is revelation. Torah, by its content and its nature, encompasses all of God-given knowledge. Torah must then include, in the words of Brigham Young, even the alphabet and even the multiplication tables. (We have in Judaism, indeed in theologies based upon revelations developed through studies of the letters of the alphabet and of numbers, the foundations of all learning. So the correspondence is not merely rhetorical or metaphorical.)

II

Religions say the same thing in different ways. Let us ask, when Judaism states, "The study of Torah—revelation—outweighs all else," and when The Church of Jesus Christ of Latter-day Saints says, "The glory of God is intelligence," what is it that the two affirm about the nature of the human being and of God? The answer begins in the scripture, *Let us make man in our likeness.* Judaism maintains that that part of man which is like God is not the corporeal, but the spiritual, aspect of man. Man is made in God's image. And that part of man which is like God is the thing which separates man from beast: the mind, consciousness. When man uses his mind, he is acting like God. So all things begin in consciousness and self-consciousness.

Judaism's conception of man is this: We think, therefore, we and what we do are worth taking seriously. We respond to reason and subject ourselves to discipline founded upon criticism. Our response consists in self-consciousness about all we do, think, and say. To be sure, man is dual. We are twin-things, ready to do evil and ready to do good. As the talmudic warning about not interrupting one's study even to admire a tree—that is, nature—makes clear, man cannot afford even for one instant to break off from consciousness, to open ourselves to what appears then to be "natural"; to be mindless is to lose touch with revealed order and revealed law, the luminous disciplines of the sacred. It follows from this viewpoint that, when we use our minds, we not only serve God, we also act like God. The imitation of God through the use of the intellect, as much as through service to God's people, or through ethical behavior, or even acceptance of suffering, is hardly a common perspective in the world of religions. Yet, I think it is clear, God gives us our minds, and that which God gives us which is distinctive to us is what in us is like God.

It should be remembered that these rather general observations will be given much specificity when we consider, in the fourth lecture, precisely what we mean by using our minds, that is, what the Jew does when he or she "studies Torah"—the document one studies, the way in which one does the work. At this point, however, the theological results are given, and only later, the concrete historical and literary foundations thereof.

III

There are two further sides to the matter. First, we must ask ourselves, How can we understand the notion that when we use our minds, we imitate God? How, in Mormon words, can we maintain, "The glory of God is intelligence"? To phrase the question in the terms of Judaism, let me report that "study of Torah"—the Judaic equivalent to "intelligence" of LDS language—involves highly critical attitudes and modes of thought. Specifically, there are four ways in which any proposition, of faith or of law, will be analyzed in the pages of the Talmud, which, alongside the scriptures, is one of the principal sacred books of Judaism. These four ways are (1) abstract, rational criticism of each tradition in sequence; (2) historical criticism of sources and their relationships; (3) philological and literary criticism of the meanings of words and phrases; and (4) practical criticism of what people actually do in order to carry out their religious obligations. It goes without saying that these four modes of criticism are entirely contemporary. Careful, skeptical examination of answers posed to problems is utterly commonplace to modern men and women. Historical criticism of sources, which does not gullibly accept whatever is alleged as fact, is the beginning of historical study. Philological study of the origins and meanings of words, literary criticism of the style of expression—these are familiar. Finally, we take for granted that it is normal to examine people's actions against some large principle of behavior. These are traits of inquiry which are both Judaic and routinely modern. That is why we can understand *Talmud Torah* as an accessible human experience, relate to the idea, and find its theology relevant to our own situation, even though it is not that of classical Judaism. Modern men and women use their minds in those ways in which Judaic men and women who study Torah use theirs. But the latter deem that use of mind to constitute an act of liturgy—work in the name and for the sake of God.

What makes these ways of thinking different from modern modes of thought, then, is the remarkable claim that, in the give and take of argument, in the processes of criticism, we do something transcendent, more than this-worldly. I cannot overemphasize how remarkable is the combination of rational criticism and the supernatural value attached to that criticism. We simply cannot understand Judaism without confronting the other-worldly context in which this so completely secular mode of thinking goes forward. The claim is that, in seeking reason and order, we serve God.

But what are we to make of that claim? Does lucid thinking bring heavenly illumination? Perhaps the best answer may be sought in our own experience. Whence comes insight? Having put everything together in a logical and orderly way, we sometimes find ourselves immobilized. We know something, but we do not know what it means, what it suggests beyond itself. But then sometimes we catch an unexpected insight. We come in some mysterious way to a comprehension of a whole which exceeds the sum of its parts. And we cannot explain how we have seen what, in a single instant, stuns us by its ineluctable rightness, fittingness—by the unearned insight, the inexplicable understanding. For the rabbis of Judaism, that stunning moment of rational insight comes with *siyyata dishamaya*, the help of heaven. The charisma imparted by the rabbinic imagina-

4

tion to the brilliant man is not different in substance from the moral authority and spiritual dignity imparted by contemporary intellectuals to the great minds of the age. The profound honor to be paid to the intellectual paragons—the explorers of the unknown, the men and women with courage to doubt the accepted truths of the hour—is not much different from the deference shown by the disciple to the rabbi. So the religious experience of the rabbi and the secular experience of the intellectual differ not in external character. They gravely differ in the ways by which we explain and account for that experience.

It follows that the religious intellectual, Mormon or Jewish, pursues the disciplines of the intellect in the same skeptical and critical spirit as does the non-religious intellectual. But the religious intellectual understands that, when there is insight, when the parts add up to more than the sum of the whole, then our minds have achieved that which is transcendent. The moment of inexplicable understanding, of rational insight, in which things fall together into a whole, to us is a moment of revelation. And, we believe, it is God who reveals insight and truth: "The glory of God is intelligence."

IV

Once we confront the notion that, when we use our minds, we enter the world of transcendence, we then have to ask, What is at the center of the intellectual task? To answer this question, we turn back to the words of Brigham Young to Brother Maeser: "I want you to remember that you ought not to teach even the alphabet or the multiplication tables without the Spirit of God." Judaism, for its part, maintains that—for a reason I shall explain—the study of Torah encompasses each and every aspect of life. It will follow that one cannot study the alphabet or the multiplication tables without learning something about the world which is the Lord's. The ultimate task of study of Torah is not solely ethical. It is holiness. To be sure, one must do the good, but Torah encompasses more than ethical behavior. The good is more than the moral; it is also the well-regulated conduct of matters to which morality is impertinent. The whole man, private and public, is to be disciplined. For no limits are set to the methods of exploring reason and searching for order. Social order with its concomitant ethical concern is no more important than the psychic order of the individual, with its full articulation in the "ritual" life. All reality comes under the discipline of the critical intellect; all is capable of sanctification.

This brings me to the issue I alluded to a moment ago. Why is it that, for Judaism, the study of Torah encompasses each and every aspect of life? Or why is it that the whole of a university faculty, in all areas and subjects, may be deemed at Brigham Young University to participate in the study of revelation? Let me begin by speaking of the Judaic tradition alone, then generalize the frame of reference. The single-minded pursuit of unifying truths about all reality constitutes the primary intellectual discipline of Judaism. But the discipline does not derive from the secular and inductive perception of unifying order in the natural world. Order comes, rather, from the lessons imparted supernaturally by revelation, that is, in the Torah. The sages perceive the Torah not as a melange of sources and laws of different origins, but as a single, unitary document, a corpus of laws reflective of an underlying ordered will. The Torah reveals the way things are meant to be, just as the rabbis' formulation and presentation of their laws tell how things are meant to be, whether or not that is how they actually are done. Order derives from the plan and will of the Creator of the world, the foundation of all reality. The Torah is interpreted by the talmudic rabbis to be the architect's design for reality: God looked into the Torah and created the world, just as an architect follows his prior design in raising a building. A single, whole Torah underlies the one, seamless reality of the world. The search for the unities hidden by the pluralities of the trivial world, the supposition that some one thing is revealed by many things—these represent, in intellectual form, the theological and metaphysical conception of a single, unique God, creator of heaven and earth, revealer of one complete Torah, guarantor of the unity and ultimate meaning of all the human actions and events that constitute history. On that account the Talmud links the private deeds of man to a larger pattern, provides a large and general "meaning" for small, particular, trivial doings.

Behind this conception of the unifying role of reason and the integrating force of criticism lies the conviction that God supplies the model for man's mind, therefore man, through reasoning in the Torah's laws, may penetrate into God's intent and plan. The rabbis of the Talmud believe they study Torah as God does in heaven; their schools—they maintain—are conducted like the academy on high. They perform rites just as God performs rites, wearing fringes as does he, putting on phylacteries just as God puts on phylacteries. In studying Torah they beseech the heavenly paradigm revealed by God "in his image," handed down from Moses and the prophets to their own teachers.

If the rabbis of the Talmud study and realize the divine teachings of Moses, whom they call "our rabbi," it is because the order they impose upon earthly affairs replicates on earth the order they perceive from heaven, the rational reconstruction of reality. It is Torah which reveals the mind of God, the principles by which he shaped reality. So studying Torah is not merely imitating God, who does the same, but is a way to the apprehension of God and the attainment of the sacred. The modes of argument are holy because they lead from earth to heaven, as prayer or fasting or self-denial cannot. Reason is the way, God's way. The holy man is therefore he who is able to think clearly and penetrate profoundly into that reality corresponding to the mysteries of the Torah. And, as I have pointed out, since revelation concerns the creation of the world and tells us its purpose and meaning, whatever intellectual efforts uncover the character of creation and bring us closer to the Creator and ourselves constitute a vehicle of revelation.

V

It follows that the belief that one God made the world lays before the Jewish religious intellectual the work of discovering the order of the well-ordered existence and well-correlated relationships. The prevalent attitude of *Talmud Torah* is perfect seriousness (not specious solemnity) about life, man's intentions, and his actions. The presupposition of the Judaic approach to life is that order is better than chaos, reflection than whim, decision than accident, and rationality than witlessness and force. The only admissible force is the power of logic, refined against the gross matter of daily living. The sole purpose is so to construct the discipline of everyday life and to pattern the relationships among men that all things are intelligible, well-regulated, trustworthy—and thereby sanctified. Judaism stands for the subjection of life to rational study.

For nothing is so trivial as to be unrelated to some conceptual, abstract principle. All things are subject to critical analysis. But the mode of inquiry is not man's alone. As I said, man is made in God's image. And that part of man which is like God is not corporeal. It is the thing which separates man from beast: the mind, consciousness. When man uses his mind, he is acting like God. That surely is a conviction uncharacteristic of modern intellectuals. Yet it is at the heart of Judaic intellectuality.

This brings me to yet another dictum on the religious value of education, Brigham Young's saying, "Education is the power to think clearly, the power to act well in the world's work, and the power to appreciate life." I think the power to think clearly is best expressed, in Judaic modes of thought, through the perpetual skepticism which is characteristic of Talmudic modes of argument. This is expressed in response to every declarative sentence or affirmative statement. Once one states that matters are so, it is inevitable that he will find as a response: "Why do you think so?" or "Perhaps things are the opposite of what you say?" or "How can you say so when a contrary principle may be adduced?" Articulation, forthrightness, subtle reasoning but lucid expression, skepticism—these are the traits of intellectuals, not of untrained and undeveloped minds, nor of neat scholars, capable only to serve as curators of the past, but not as critics of the present.

Above all, Judaic thinking at its best rejects gullibility and credulity. It is, indeed, peculiarly modern in its systematic skepticism, its testing of each proposition, not to destroy but to refine what people suppose to be so. The Talmud's first question, for example, is not "Who says so?" but "Why?" "What is the reason?" Faith is restricted to ultimate matters, to the fundamental principles of reality beyond which one may not penetrate. But humility in the face of ultimate questions is not confused with servility before the assertions, the truth-claims, of authorities, ancient or modern, who are no more than mortal.

The way to deeper perception lies in skepticism about shallow assertion. One must place as small a stake as possible in the acceptance of specific allegations. The fewer vested convictions, the greater the chances for wide-ranging inquiry. But while modern skepticism may yield—at least in the eye of its critics—corrosive and negative results, in the Talmud, skepticism produces measured restraint and limited insight. The difference must be in the open-endedness of the Talmudic inquiry: nothing is ever left as a final answer, a completed solution. The fruit of insight is inquiry; the result of inquiry is insight, in endless progression. The only road closed is the road back, to the unarticulated, the unconscious, and the unself-conscious. For once consciousness is achieved, a reason spelled out, one cannot again pretend there is no reason, and nothing has been articulated. For the Talmud the alternatives are not faith or nihilism, but reflection or dumb reflex, consciousness or animal instinct. Man, in God's image, has the capacity to reflect and to criticize. All an animal can do is act and respond.

That is why energy, the will to act, has to be channeled and controlled by intellect: *You are what you do.* Therefore, deed without deliberation is not to be taken seriously. Examination of deeds takes priority over mere repetition of what works or what feels good. For this purpose, genius is insufficient; cleverness is irrelevant. What is preferred is systematic and orderly consideration, step by step, of the principles by which one acts. The human problem in the Judaic conception is not finding the motive force to do, but discovering the restraint to regulate that protean force. In the quest for restraint and self-control, the primal energies will insure one is not bored or lacking in purpose. For the Judaic mode of thought perceives a perpetual tension between energy and activity, on the one side, and reflection on the other. To act without thought comes naturally, is contrary, therefore, to the fact of revealed discipline. The drama of the private life consists in the struggle between will and intellect, action and reflection. If Judaism is on the side of the intellect and reflection, it is because the will and action require no allies. The outcome will be determined, ultimately, by force of character and intellect, these together. And the moot issue is not how to repress, but how to reshape the primal energy.

VI

If then I have to summarize the purpose of the intellectual life in Judaism, it is that use of mind is the search for what is sacred. The Talmud, for its part, endures as a monument to intellectualism focused upon the application of practical rationality to society. It pays tribute, on every page, to the human potential to think morally, yet without lachrymose sentimentality, to reflect about fundamentals and basic principles, yet for concrete purposes and with ordinary society in mind. The good, well-regulated society will nurture disciplined, strong character. The mighty man—"one who overcomes his impulses"—will stand as a pillar of the good society. This is what I understand as the result of the intellectual activity of the moral intellect. Reason, criticism, restraint and rational exchange of ideas—these are the things Judaism requires of the mind.

Now for contemporary man Judaism presents formidable criticism, for by it the value, "follow your own impulse"—utter subjectivism in all things—is rejected. Judaism gives contrary advice. "Tame your impulse," regulate, restrain, control energies through the self-imposition of the restraining rule of law. At the same time, Judaism demands that a person *not* do "his own thing" alone, but persuade others to make what is his own into what is to be shared by all. Judaism therefore subjects the individual to restraints on his pure individuality, while opening for individuality the possibility of moral suasion of the community at large. "Unrestrained" and "individualism" therefore are set over against "regulated" and "rationality." For it is rationality which overcomes the isolation of the individual, connecting one mind to another through the mediating way of reason. Through the imposition of rational, freely adopted rules, one restrains those destructive elements of the personality which are potentially damaging for both the individual and the community.

What makes this theory of the intellect as an instrument of sanctification relevant to modern men and women is a trait of mind of contemporary people, which is, as I said, their pragmatism and willingness to cope with details and to take seriously the trivialities of ordinary life. Because of this very secularity, the seriousness about worldly things characteristic of our own day, we are able to understand the importance of Judaism's lessons about the criticism and regulation of worldly things. What shall we say of a tradition of thought that lays greatest emphasis upon deed, upon a pattern of actions and a way of living, but that is pragmatic? What shall we say of a perspective upon the world that focuses on practical reason, but that is worldly? What shall we conclude of a religious language that calls honesty or charity a *qiddush hashem*, a sanctification of God's name, but that is deeply secular? A legal system whose deepest concerns are for the detailed articulation of the this-worldly meaning of love for one's fellow human beings here and now is one which long ago brought the Jews into the pragmatic, this-worldly framework of modernity. But with them the Jews brought their conception of religious ontology, which holds that the secular is susceptible to the sanctification to be effected by the human being. The ontology of modernity and that of pragmatic Jewry are hardly identical.

That is why Judaism and its Talmud not only relate to the contemporary world, but stand in judgment of it. And both the Judaic and the Mormon religions surely will judge a world willing to reduce man to part of himself, to impulses and energies. They will judge an age prepared to validate the unrestrained expression of those energies as the ultimate, legitimate adumbration of what is individual about the person, as though he had no mind, no strength of rational thought. They will condemn a world of enthusiasts who make an improvement and call it redemption, come up with a good idea and, without the test of skeptical analysis, pronounce salvation. Judaism shows a better way: It demonstrates that men have the capacity to assess the unredemption of the world, to perceive the tentativeness of current solutions to enduring problems, and at the same time to hope for sanctification and to work for salvation. It is this unfulfilled yet very vivid evaluation of the world, the power to take the world so seriously as to ask searching questions about its certainties which, I think, explains the Jew's capacity to love so much, and yet to doubt: to hold the world very near and close, with open arms. The Jew has been taught to engage realistically in the world's tasks, to do so with a whole heart, yet without the need, or even the power, to regard completion of those tasks as the threshold of a final and completed fulfillment of history. Because of its mode of thinking, Judaism teaches men to take seriously the wide range of worldly problems without expecting that in solving them—provisionally, let alone finally—they might save the world.

VII

But to serve the world through the intellect, we have to consider what makes our modes of thought more than merely an expression of practical reason, but rather, an expression of the transcendent which is in ourselves. The world cannot ask our respective religions to vindicate themselves by *its* standards. We have to bring to bear upon the world's perceptions the sacred images of us imparted to us by our respective religions. Let me at the end say what the Judaic perspective is, what Judaism's sacred image of us may be. To begin with, Judaism asks, What say you of the human condition? What is man, but that God is mindful of him? If all we are and ever shall be is here and now, if our minds are merely useful and if our capacity to think entirely a secular virtue, then the Judaic mode of intellect is unavailable to us. If through our strength of reason we pursue the profound rationality which underlies, gives unity, and imparts meaning to, existence, and if through our power of reflection we then undertake the reconstruction of reality, the interpretation of what is in terms of what can and should be, then we shall have already entered into the Judaic situation. But when we do, we shall thereby have undertaken all that Judaism knows as the discipline of the sacred. We shall, in other words, have renewed the experience of sanctification both *through* the intellect and *of* the intellect. That experience becomes consequential when the godly perceptions of life and interpretations of society come to possess us. I therefore speak, without shame, of religious experience, indeed of the turning toward God which the sages called *teshuvah*, insufficiently translated as repentance, but truly meaning *turning*. The way of Judaic piety and spirituality has been the path of saints—saints of former times and of these days—a path each chooses and may choose again, in full rationality, at life's turning.

2

Cultic Piety and Pharisaism Before 70

T he theology of Torah-learning, so important in Judaism from the end of ancient times to our own day, emerges in the pages of the Babylonian Talmud and certainly speaks for the rabbis of the late second through the seventh centuries and beyond. But at what point in the history of Judaism does the ideal of Torah-learning enter the theological arena of Judaism? Under whose auspices do we find that ideal shaped into the important component of normative Judaic theology? The answers to these questions are assumed in nearly all accounts of the history of Judaism to be as follows: the rabbis of the Talmud are the heirs and continuators of the Pharisees of the period before 70. Since the ideal of Torah-learning is central to the theology of the talmudic rabbis, it surely derives from, and wholly characterizes, the Pharisees. And, it follows, wherever we find references, in connection with the Pharisees, to a corpus of "traditions of the fathers," what we have is none other than those Torah-traditions, now found in Mishnah and called "Oral Torah," traditions which are the focus of the activity of Torah-learning. It follows that the Pharisees are represented as a group formed around the ideal of Torah-learning, and that their principal interest lay in the interpretation of scriptures and their application to contemporary affairs.

In my view, that picture is not correct. My argument now unfolds in two parts. In the present lecture, I shall discuss what it is that the sources do tell us about the Pharisees. The next then will deal with the beginnings of the ideal of Torah-learning and with the context in which the ideal takes shape as a theological norm, which in my view, is the period after 70. So let us first ask, Are the Pharisees represented as a sect devoted to the preservation and mastery of Torah-traditions? What, in fact, do the sources describe as the center of Pharisaic piety?

I

Information on the Pharisees before 70 comes from three sources, all of which reached their present state after that date: first, allusions to the Pharisees in the works of Josephus; second, references to relationships between the Pharisees and Jesus occurring in the Gospels produced by Christian communities between 70 and 100; third, laws and sayings attributed to, and stories told about, the Pharisees by the rabbis from the period following 70 and contained in the Mishnah and Tosefta, ca. 200, and later collections. These three sources are different in character. The first are found in a systematic, coherent historical narrative. The second are in collections of stories and sayings, whose polemical tendency *vis à vis* the Pharisees is readily discernible. The third consists chiefly of laws and stories arranged according to legal categories in codes and in commentaries on those codes over a period of four hundred years and more after 70. The purpose of Josephus is to explain that Rome was not at fault for the destruction of the Temple and that the Jews were misled in fighting Rome. The Gospels' interest is in the life and teaching of Jesus. The rabbinical legislators promulgated laws of the administration of the Jewish community. To none were the historical character and doctrines of the Pharisees of primary concern. Much that we are told about them anachronistically reflects the situation and interests of the writers, not of the historical Pharisees. Pharisaic theology before 70 is particularly difficult to recover, because the later rabbinical documents do not distinguish the ideas of the Pharisees before that date from those of second- and third-

political life. But, strikingly, Josephus makes no reference to the group's functioning *as a party* within the revolutionary councils. We may conclude that Simeon and others were members of the pharisaic group, but not the group's representatives, any more than Judah the Pharisee represented the pharisaic *group* in founding the Fourth Philosophy. The Pharisees, then, probably did not constitute an organized political force. Evidently the end of the pharisaic political party came with Aristobulus II, who slaughtered many of them; so far as Josephus is concerned, after this the Pharisees as a group played no important role in the politics and government of Jewish Palestine.

The Pharisees are represented as a philosophical school by Josephus, who thought of groups in Jewish society distinguished by peculiar theories and practices as different schools of the national philosophy. When they were a political party, the Pharisees probably claimed that they ought to rule because they possessed true and wise doctrines. The specific doctrines ascribed to them, however, seem quite unrelated to the political aspirations of the group. It is not clear why people who believe in fate and in the immortality of the soul should rule or would rule differently from those who did not, nor is it clear how such beliefs might shape the policies of the state. These are matters of interest to Greek readers, to be sure. But evidently what characterized the group—these *particular* beliefs—and what rendered their political aspirations something more than a power-grab were inextricably related, at least in the eyes of their contemporaries.

Josephus thus presents us with a party of philosophical politicians. He gives us no hint as to the origin or early history of the Pharisees. In fact we have no information on that question from any source. The Pharisees claim to have ancient traditions, but these are not described by Josephus as having been orally transmitted, or attributed to Moses at Sinai, or claimed as part of the Torah. Nor is the study of such traditions represented as important in their piety. Josephus says they were excellent lawyers, marked off from other groups by a few philosophical differences. As a party they functioned effectively for roughly the first fifty years of the first century B.C. While individuals thereafter are described as Pharisees, the group seems to end its political life as a sect before the advent of Herod.

III

The generally negative picture of the Pharisees given by the New Testament produced, in the later history of the West, a highly partisan caricature. "Pharisee" became a synonym for hypocrite, as in the *Shorter Oxford English Dictionary:*

> *Pharisee:* One of an ancient Jewish sect distinguished by their strict observance of the traditional and written law, and by their pretensions to superior sanctity. A person of this disposition; a self-righteous person; a formalist; a hypocrite.

Historical research lacks adequate sources to verify or refute these assertions. We do not have diaries, for example, to permit us to compare what a Pharisee said publicly against what he said in private and so to ascertain whether or not he was a hypocrite. Nor are we able to assess with impartiality the claim that a Pharisee is "self-righteous." Clearly, "pretensions to superior sanctity" are relative. If one concedes the correctness of a theological claim, then one will not regard it as "pretension." Nor do we know of what that claim to "superior sanctity" would have consisted.

When we discount the hostile polemic, however, we do find in the New Testament a number of important assertions. The Pharisees are represented in the main, though not entirely, as a table-fellowship sect. While Mark 3:6 and 12:13, for instance, represent the Pharisees as allies of the Herodians, thus as a political sect of some sort, they are characterized, particularly in sayings attributed to Jesus, as a group of people who keep the same dietary laws and therefore may eat together. Pharisaic table-fellowship required keeping under all circumstances the laws of purity that normally applied only in the Jerusalem Temple, so that the Pharisees ate their private meals in the same condition of ritual purity as did the priests of the cult. The Pharisees laid further stress upon proper tithing of foods and Sabbath observance. The Gospels say much else about the Pharisees, but these are the main points that survive when we discount the polemic which informs the Gospels.

The Gospels' stories about the Pharisees are set in the first forty years of the first century A.D. and derive from the second half of the century, between ca. 70 and ca. 100. The Evangelists assume a violently antagonistic view of the Pharisees. At the same time, the Pharisees are represented by Acts as a major force in the government of the Jewish community. One learns much in the synoptic traditions, John, and Acts about the attitudes of the early Christian community toward the Pharisees and the relationships of the Pharisees toward the Christians. Viewed as an autonomous sect, and not in relationship to the early Church, however, the Pharisees are of no great interest to New Testament writers. The first evidence on Pharisaism derives from Paul, who describes himself "as to the law, a Pharisee" (Philippians 3:5), and "extremely zealous for the traditions of my fathers." (Galatians 1:14.) Acts 22:3 has Paul claim he was brought up in Jerusalem "at the feet of Gamaliel" and that he lived as a Pharisee (Acts 26:4), which in context is joined to the belief in the resurrection of the dead. The substance of Paul's pharisaism in Philippians and Galatians is not made clear. If one important aspect was preserving purity outside of the Temple, then Paul could not have been a Pharisee abroad, in Tarsus, for foreign territory was by definition unclean. In that case his upbringing in Jerusalem will have made possible his adherence to the party. The narrative of Acts leaves no doubt, however, that included in pharisaic doctrine was belief in the resurrection of the dead.

In the Synoptic Gospels and John we may discern five kinds of materials pertinent to pharisaism: first, those in which the Pharisees are represented as enemies of Jesus, forming part of the narrative background; second, and closely related, material in which the Pharisees criticize Jesus; third, those in which pharisaic hypocrisy is condemned in general terms; fourth, those representing Pharisees and Christians in agreement, either on general or on particular matters of doctrine; and, finally, materials in which the Pharisees are condemned for specific practices or beliefs. This last sort of material is of greatest interest, and we turn directly to it because of its attention to details of the Pharisees' actual beliefs and practices, primarily as they pertain to conduct at meals. What the Pharisees do, and what Jesus does not do, when enjoying table-fellowship, comprise the subject of important stories. In quantity and character these materials exhibit important differences from the rest. Jesus and his disciples eat with sinners and tax collectors, people who do not keep the law. (Mark 2:15-23; Matthew 9:10-17.) It is unlikely that these people observe the laws of ritual purity at meals or tithe their food. Rabbinic law explicitly excludes tax collectors from table-fellowship of the *haburah*. (Tos. Demai 3:4.) The question of fasting is raised. The Pharisees fast, but the Christians do not. (Mark 2:15-23.) Jesus is made to explain that fact. Another issue is preparation of food on the Sabbath (Mark 2:15-28; Matthew 12:1-14): Is it permissible to harvest food on the Sabbath? The story is generated by the saying, "The Son of Man is lord of the Sabbath," and the Pharisees are not central to the account.

The most interesting group of stories explicitly concerns ritual purity in eating. The Christian disciples do not wash their hands. The details of the ritual purity laws are unknown. Mark assumed that his reader would not understand that in general the Pharisees and all the Jews wash their hands before meals, and wash cups, pots, and bronze vessels. (Mark 7:1-13.) This is all regarded as part of the "tradition of the elders," which the Gospels and Josephus assign to the Pharisees. But one would not have to know a great deal about Pharisaic purity rules to know that the Pharisees maintained such practices. The narrator obviously has little more to report than that simple fact. His purpose is to contrast purity rules with ethical laws, for one is claimed to be in conflict with the other. The question of ritual defilement through the eating of food also is raised. This is not merely a matter of prohibited foods, such as not eating pork or certain kinds of fish, but concerns cultic purity. The moral character of the Pharisees is further criticized. While they keep the ritual purity laws, they neglect other important precepts of the Torah, and are therefore incapable of bringing men to salvation. The most important *detail* in the polemic against ritual tithing: Pharisees tithe their food, but neglect "the weightier matters of the law, justice and mercy and faith." (Mark 7:1-13; Matthew 15:1-20; Luke 11:37-41.) But then Jesus is made to say that there is no conflict between the one and the other.

Mark claims that Jesus annulled the pharisaic purity-rite of hand-washing before the common meal, declaring it the "tradition of men." Then, as an entirely separate issue, Mark 7:14ff. has Jesus allude to the defilement of foods. Nothing which goes into a man from outside can defile him—"Thus he declared all foods clean."

(Mark 7:19.) Mark carefully distinguishes purity of hands from purity of food. The one is a human invention, the other is scriptural, but has not been correctly interpreted by the Pharisees. Matthew, by contrast, leaves out Mark 7:19. He follows Mark in claiming the washing of hands is not a divine commandment (Matthew 15:1-3), and separately treats the cleanness of foods. (Matthew 15:10-19.) But then, ignoring their differences—the hand-washing as a Pharisaic custom, the food as a biblical injunction—Matthew links the two in a curious fusion (Matthew 15:20): "These [iniquitous deeds] are what defile a man, but to eat with unwashed hands does not defile a man." Mark was appropriately silent on the supposed connection between the customary washing of the hands and the Mosaic rules on the cleanness of foods. Matthew has confused them. By contrast, Mark has correctly kept the two matters separated: washing was never part of the Torah, but was a pharisaic custom; food-laws were meant to teach a moral lesson, not to be interpreted in a literal way.

Matthew 23:25 (Luke 11:39-41) and 23:27-8 take up and develop the contrast between inside and outside. The Pharisees clean the outside of the cup and plate, but inside are full of extortion. Similarly, the scribes and Pharisees are like whitewashed tombs, outwardly beautiful but inwardly full of uncleanness. The contrast between impurity and iniquity, on the one side, and purity and righteousness, on the other, is commonplace. What is more interesting is the problem of the division of the parts of the cup into insides and outsides. For Jesus these serve as a metaphor for inner against outer purity. What is to be kept pure is the inside of the man, a play on the theme introduced in connection with the cleanness of foods. Later rabbinic law distinguished between the inside of the cup, which was highly susceptible to ritual impurity, and which, when unclean, rendered the whole cup unclean, and the outside, which was less susceptible and would not impart purity to the inside. But that fact is unimportant in the interpretation of Jesus' saying. To be sure, Jesus takes the strict view that the outside had to be clean. But the whole saying is solely a metaphor for moral purity and is not built upon exact knowledge of the possibly later purity-rule. If Jesus was supposed to have known the rule and to have treated it literally, he could not have told the Pharisees first to cleanse the inside of the cup. That was their rule to begin with. The figurative sense is lost if one really does clean the inside of the cup first of all.

The Gospels' account of the pharisaic critique of Jesus focuses on three issues. First, why do Jesus' disciples eat with tax collectors? Second, why do Jesus' disciples not fast? Third, why does Jesus violate the Sabbath by healing on the holy day? The third theme recurs in the specific critique of the Pharisees. The general condemnation is composed of mere invective: the Pharisees are a "brood of vipers"; one should beware of the "leaven" of the Pharisees "which is hypocrisy." Pharisees love money. Pharisees regard themselves as better than other men by reason of their religious observances. The important data derive not from the polemical narrative materials, but from the condemnation of the Pharisees for specific religious practices. The most interesting information comes from Mark 7:1-23, on ritual purity in eating and on the dietary laws, and Matthew 23:1-36, on the Pharisees' emphasis on ritual purity of dishes and their exact tithing. These passages take for granted specific pharisaic rites, and direct criticism against them. They tell us not only that the early Christian community found itself in conflict with the pharisaic party, but that Pharisees known to the Gospel story-tellers carried out important rites which are quite relevant to the doctrinal issues, important to the Christians, in the Pharisaic-Christian relationship.

IV

Rabbinic traditions redacted long after 70 refer to masters who lived before that time. These masters are listed, for example in Mishnah Hagigah 2:2, as patriarch (Nasi) and head of the court (Ab Bet Din). We have in addition the names of very few masters whom rabbinic traditions evidently believe to have lived before 70. We take for granted that those named in Mishnah Hagigah 2:2 and other authorities included in pericopae along with the patriarchs and heads of the court down to 70 were Pharisees.[1] We are on firm ground in making that assumption, for at least two of the names on

---

1. Professor Sarason comments, "provided that the list is not a schematic homogenization of diverse names."

the list, Gamaliel and Simeon b. Gamaliel, are referred to as Pharisees in non-rabbinic sources, Acts 5:34 for Gamaliel, Josephus's *Life* (190, 216, 309) for Simeon, his son. The rabbinic traditions about the Pharisees consist of approximately 371 separate items—stories, sayings, or allusions—different versions of which occur in approximately 655 different pericopae, or completed units of tradition. Of these, 280 items in 462 pericopae (comprising about 75 percent of the total), pertain to Hillel and people associated with Hillel, such as Shammai and the Houses of Hillel and Shammai.

Insofar as we know it, pharisaic law comprises those legal sayings in talmudic literature attributed either to pharisaic masters before 70 or to the Houses of Shammai and Hillel. A legal saying is a statement of what one must or must not do, commonly in everyday life. It may pertain to the adjudication of civil disputes, the conduct of the Temple cult, the manner of issuing a writ of divorce, the way to say one's prayers, to tithe food, to preserve ritual purity, or to purify something which has been defiled or made unclean. Pharisaic laws pertained to a wide range of mostly commonplace matters. Most of the nearly 700 pericopae pertaining to Pharisees before 70 concern legal matters, and the larger number of these relate to, first, agricultural tithes, offerings, and other taboos, and, second, rules of ritual purity—that is, rules of sectarian interest.

Purity predominates in the pharisaic laws. Purity was the center of sectarian controversy. The Pharisees were Jews who believed that the purity laws were to be kept outside of the Temple. Other Jews, following the plain sense of Leviticus, supposed that purity laws were to be kept only in the Temple, where the priests had to enter a state of ritual purity in order to carry out such requirements as animal sacrifice. They likewise had to eat their Temple food in a state of ritual purity, while lay people did not. To be sure, everyone who went to the Temple had to be ritually pure. But outside of the Temple the laws of ritual purity were not observed, for it was not required that non-cultic activities be conducted in a state of Levitical cleanness.

But the Pharisees held that even outside of the Temple, in one's own home, the laws of ritual purity were to be followed in the only circumstances in which they might apply, namely, at the table. Therefore, one must eat secular food (ordinary everyday meals) in a state of ritual purity as if one were a Temple priest. The Pharisees thus arrogated to themselves—and to all Jews equally—the status of the Temple priests. We assume so because they performed actions restricted to priests on account of their status, specifically by eating ordinary food in Levitical purity. The table of every Jew in his home therefore was seen as being like the table of the Lord in the Jerusalem Temple. The commandment, "You shall be a kingdom of priests and a holy people" evidently was taken literally: everyone is a priest, everyone stands in the same relationship to God, and everyone must keep the priestly laws. At this time, only the Pharisees held such a viewpoint, and eating unconsecrated food as if one were a Temple priest at the Lord's table was thus one of the two things a person had to do as a Pharisee. The other was meticulous tithing. The laws of tithing and related agricultural taboos may have been kept primarily by Pharisees. Our evidence here is less certain. Pharisees clearly regarded keeping the agricultural rules as a chief religious duty. But whether, to what degree, and how other Jews did so is not clear. But the agricultural laws and purity rules in the end affected table-fellowship. They were "dietary laws."

If the Pharisees were primarily a group for Torah-study, as the Dead Sea Scrolls' writers describe themselves, then we should have expected more rules about the school, perhaps also about scribal matters. In fact, we have only one, about sneezing in the schoolhouse. Surely other more fundamental problems ought to have presented themselves. Neither do we find much interest in defining the master-disciple relationship, including the duties of the master and the responsibilities and rights of the disciple, the way in which the disciple should learn his lessons, and similar matters of importance in later times. The exception to this rule is the sayings in the Sayings of the Fathers (*Pirqé Abot*). They do refer to Torah-study and discipleship. Those sayings, attributed to masters before 70, are first attested in the third century. No one before that time alludes to any of them, while numerous other traditions attributed to masters who lived before 70 elicit comments from authorities from 70 to the editing of the Mishnah in ca. 200. This strongly suggests that the Torah sayings of *Abot* have been attributed anachronistically to the Pharisees before 70.

This brings us to a puzzling fact: nowhere in the rabbinic

traditions of the Pharisees do we find a reference to gatherings for ritual meals, or table-fellowship, of the pharisaic party, apart from an allusion to the meeting of several *haburot* (fellowship groups) in the same hall. This surely supplies a slender basis on which to prove that the pharisaic party actually conducted communion meals, especially since no pharisaic ritual meal is ever mentioned. By contrast, the Qumran laws, which make much of purity, also refer to communion meals and the right or denial of the right of access to them. The whole editorial and redactional framework of the rabbinical traditions is silent about ritual meals and table-fellowship. The narrative materials say nothing on the matter. No stories are told about how the "rabbis" were eating together, when such-and-such was said. The redactional formula for pharisaic sayings never alludes to a meal as the setting for a given saying. So the laws concentrate attention on rules and regulations covering all aspects of a ritual meal. But the myth or rites of such a meal are never described or even alluded to. The pharisaic group evidently did not conduct table-fellowship meals *as rituals*. The table-fellowship laws pertained not merely to group life, but to daily life quite apart from a sectarian setting and ritual occasion. The rules applied to the home, not merely to the synagogue or Temple. While the early Christians gathered for special ritual meals which became the climax of their group life, the Pharisees apparently did not.

The very character of the Pharisees' sectarianism therefore differs from that of the Christians. While the communion-meal embodied and actualized sectarian life for the Christians, the expression of the Pharisees' sense of self-awareness as a group apparently was not a similarly intense ritual meal. Eating was not a ritualized occasion, even though the Pharisees had liturgies to be said at the meal. No communion ceremony, no rites centered on meals, no specification of meals on holy occasions characterize pharisaic table-fellowship. The one communion-meal about which we find legislation characterized all sects, along with the rest of the Jews: the Passover *Seder*. The Pharisees *may* have had *Seder* rules separate from, and in addition to, those observed by everyone else. But these hardly prove they held a communion-meal.

Pharisaic table-fellowship, therefore, was a quite ordinary, everyday affair. The various fellowship rules had to be observed in wholly routine daily circumstances, without accompanying rites other than a benediction for the food. The Christians' myths and rituals rendered table-fellowship into a much heightened spiritual experience: *"Do this in memory of me."* The Pharisees told no stories about purity laws, except (in later times) to account for their historical development (e.g., who had decreed which purity rule?). When they came to table, so far as we know, they told no stories about how Moses had done what they now do, and they did not "do these things in memory of Moses our rabbi." The sect ordinarily did not gather as a *group* at all. All their meals required ritual purity. Pharisaic table-fellowship took place in the same circumstances as did all non-ritual table-fellowship. Members of the sect were engaged in workaday pursuits like everyone else. This fact made the actual purity rules and food restrictions all the more important, for keeping the law alone set the Pharisees apart from the people among whom they lived. Not in the wilderness, on festivals, or on Sabbaths alone, but on weekdays and in the towns, without telling myths, or reading holy books (Torah-talk at table is attested to only later), or reenacting first things, pharisaic table-fellowship depended solely on observance of the cultic law and expressed a piety formed on the analogy to that of the cult. The relevance of all this to the point at which *Talmud Torah* becomes the central Judaic symbol and action is negative: We cannot look to the Pharisees of the period before 70 for the source of the ideal and the motive for its serving as the center for Judaic piety.

3

From Cultic Piety to
Torah-Piety After 70

A s I shall now show, the destruction of the Temple marks the shift from cultic piety to Torah-piety, that is, from the conception that the holy life consists in imitating at ordinary meals the cleanness required of the priest in the Temple, to the notion that the holy life consists in studying Torah and carrying out its requirements (commandments). Our task is to analyze this shift in the character of the central symbolic structure of that form of Judaism known to us from the rabbinic sources and assigned by them to the Pharisees before 70, hence of "Pharisaic-Rabbinic" Judaism.

To begin with, we must remind ourselves that before the destruction, there was a common "Judaism" in the land of Israel, and it was by no means identical to what we now understand as Pharisaic Judaism. We have concentrated on sects: Pharisees, Essenes, Christians. But the common religion of the country consisted of three main elements: first, the Hebrew scriptures, second, the Temple, and third, the common and accepted practices of the ordinary folk—their calendar, their mode of living, their everyday practices and rites, based on these first two. In addition, we know of a number of peculiar groups, or sects, which took a distinctive position on one or another aspect of the common, inherited religious-culture. Among these sects, the best known are the Pharisees, the Sadducees, and the Essenes; this third group, described chiefly in the writings of Josephus, exhibits traits in common with the group known to us from the so-called Dead Sea Scrolls, but cannot have been identical to it in every respect.

I

When the Temple was destroyed, it is clear, the foundations of the country's religious-cultural life were destroyed. The reason is that the Temple had constituted one of the primary, unifying elements in that common life. The structure not only of political life and of society, but also of the imaginative life of the country, depended upon the Temple and its worship and cult. It is there that people believed they served God. On the Temple the lines of structure—both cosmic and social—converged. The Temple, moreover, served as the basis for those many elements of autonomous self-government and political life left in the Jews' hands by the Romans. Consequently, the destruction of the Temple meant not merely a significant alteration in the cultic and ritual life of the Jewish people, but also a profound and far-reaching crisis in their inner and spiritual existence.

The response to the destruction of the Temple is known to us only from rabbinic materials, which underwent revisions over many centuries. But these late materials referring to earlier days—that is, fourth-century stories about first-century teachers—are serviceable, because they give evidence of how important shirts and turnings in the character of Judaism are recognized later on and given specificity and concreteness in the period in which, on firmer grounds, we conceive these changes to have taken place. One such story, about Yohanan ben Zakkai and his disciple, Joshua ben Hananiah, captures in a few words the main outline of what became of the pharisaic-rabbinic view of the destruction:

> Once, as Rabban Yohanan ben Zakkai was coming forth from Jerusalem, Rabbi Joshua followed after him and beheld the Temple in ruins.
> "Woe unto us," Rabbi Joshua cried, "that this, the

place where the iniquities of Israel were atoned for, is laid waste!"

"My son," Rabban Yohanan said to him, "be not grieved. We have another atonement as effective as this. And what is it? It is acts of loving-kindness, as it is said, *For I desire mercy and not sacrifice.* (Hosea 6:6, *Avot de Rabbi Natan,* Chap. 6).

How shall we relate the arcane rules about ritual purity to the public calamity faced by the heirs of the Pharisees at Yavneh? What connection is there between the ritual purity of the "kingdom of priests" and the atonement of sins in the Temple?

To the Yohanan ben Zakkai of this story, preserving the Temple is not an end in itself. He teaches that there is another means of reconciliation between God and Israel, so that the Temple and its cult are not decisive. What is the will of God? It is doing deeds of loving-kindness: *I desire mercy, not sacrifice* (Hosea 6:6) means to Yohanan, "We have a means of atonement as effective as the Temple, and it is doing deeds of loving-kindness." Just as willingly as men would contribute bricks and mortar for the rebuilding of a sanctuary, so they ought to contribute renunciation, self-sacrifice, love, for the building of a sacred community.

Earlier, pharisaism had held that the cleanness of the Temple should be everywhere, even in the home and the hearth. Now Yohanan is represented as teaching that sacrifice greater than the Temple must characterize the life of the community. If one is to do something for God in a time when the Temple is no more, the offering must be the gift of selfless compassion. The holy altar must be the streets and marketplaces of the world, as, formerly, the purity of the Temple had to be observed in the streets and marketplaces. But this is essentially a backward-looking solution. How do we contend with the destruction of the cult, focus of the ancient piety? There was a second perspective, the one on the future: How shall we reshape the focus of piety, so that it is relevant to the conditions of contemporary life, when there is no Temple, and when the cultic analogy is no longer evocative? Pharisaic piety in the new age evokes a certain dissonance, since it rests on the comparison between the home and the Temple—but the Temple is no more. A new shape and focus for piety are to be found.

II

The reconstruction of a viable cultural-religious existence is the outcome of the next half-century, for, between ca. 70 and ca. 120, a number of elements of the religious-cultural structure of the period before 70 were put together into a new synthesis, the synthesis we now call Rabbinic Judaism, with its stress on study of Torah as a principal expression of piety. It was in response to the disaster of the destruction that Rabbinic Judaism took shape. Part of its success lay in its capacity to claim things that had not changed at all—hence the assertion that even at the start, Moses was "our rabbi"—while making the very destruction of the Temple itself into the verification and vindication of the new structure.

Rabbinic Judaism claimed that it was possible to serve God not only through sacrifice, but also through study of Torah. There is a priest in charge of the life of the community, but a new kind of priest, the rabbi. As we saw, the old sin-offerings still may be carried out through deeds of loving-kindness. Not only so, but when the whole Jewish people will fully carry out the teachings of the Torah, then the Temple itself will be rebuilt. To be sure, the Temple will be reconstructed along lines laid out in the Torah—that is, in the whole Torah of Moses, the Torah taught by the rabbis. And, like the prophets and historians in the time of the First Destruction, the rabbis further claimed that it was because the people had sinned, that is, had not kept the Torah, that the Temple had been destroyed. So the disaster itself is made to vindicate the rabbinic teaching and to verify its truth.

III

Now let us stand back from this synthesis and ask, How was it put together? What are its primary elements? What trends or movements before 70 are represented by these elements? Two primary components in the Yavneh synthesis are to be discerned, first, the method or mode of thought of pharisaism before 70, second, the putative values of the scribal profession before 70. The former lay stress upon universal keeping of the law, so that every Jew is obligated to do what only the elite—the priests—are normally expected to accomplish. Pre-70 pharisaism thus contributed the

32

stress on the universal keeping of the law, on the pretense that all live like Temple-priests. The second component derives from the scribes, whose professional ideal stressed the study of Torah and the centrality of the learned man in the religious system.

The unpredictable, final element in the synthesis of pharisaic stress on widespread law—including ritual-law, observance, and scribal emphasis on learning—is what makes Rabbinic Judaism distinctive, and that is the conviction that the community now stands in the place of the Temple. The ruins of the cult, after all, did not mark the end of the collective life of Israel. What survived was the *people*. It was the genius of Rabbinic Judaism following upon pharisaism, to recognize that the people might reconstitute the Temple in its own collective life, just as was the case with purity before 70. Therefore the people had to be made holy, as the Temple had been holy, and the people's social life had to be sanctified as the surrogate for what had been lost. The rabbinic ideal further maintained that the rabbi served as the new priest, the study of Torah substituted for the Temple sacrifice, and deeds of loving-kindness were the social surrogate for the sin-offering, that is, personal sacrifice instead of animal sacrifice.

We see that *Talmud Torah* is only one element in the reformation of the symbolic structure of Judaism accomplished by the rabbis of the period after 70. It is part of a larger system in which study of Torah, the rabbi, the importance of moral and ethical action, all are put together into a coherent structure, upon the foundation of the people of Israel, the Jewish people, as the locus of the sacred in this world. These elements—religious behavior, religious official, religious way of life, and religious community—together form a whole and harmonious system. When we isolate *Talmud Torah*, it is only to discern how one of the several elements of the Judaic structure has been received into the whole. And in many ways, you will agree, it is the most distinctive element of the structure. The centrality of community, the importance of ethics, the authority of a religious leader qualified by learning—these are not uncommon in the religious experience of humankind. But the idea that what everyone—and not merely the virtuosi—must do to serve God is to study revelation is unusual. In my view, as I hope is clear, that notion derives from two disparate sources: the pharisaic concept that all

Israel, a kingdom of priests and a holy people, must keep the purity-laws of the Temple; and the scribal ideal of learning as a way of life. The method is pharisaic, the substance, scribal. But putting the two together quite changes what each was before. And, as is now clear, the context in which the two are put together is what accounts for the fact that they become something entirely fresh and important.

As we saw, pre-70 pharisaism is clearly defined by the Gospels' pharisaic pericopae and the rabbinic traditions about the Pharisees. Both stress the same concerns: first, eating secular food in a state of ritual purity; second, careful tithing and giving of agricultural offerings to the priest and obedience to the biblical rules and taboos concerning raising crops; third, to a lesser degree, some special laws on keeping the Sabbaths and festivals; and, finally, still less commonly, rules on family affairs. Therefore, late pharisaism—that which flourished in the last decades of the Temple's existence and which is revealed in the Gospels and in rabbinic traditions—is a cult-centered piety, which proposes to replicate the cult in the home, and thus to effect the Temple's purity laws at the table of the ordinary Jew, and quite literally to turn Israel into a "kingdom of priests and a holy nation." The symbolic structure of pharisaism depends upon that of the Temple; the ideal is the same as that of the priesthood. The Pharisee was a layman pretending to be priest and making his private home into a model of the Temple. The laws about purity and careful tithing were dietary laws, governing what and how a person should eat. If a person kept those laws, then, when he ate at home, he was like God at the Temple's altar table, on which was arrayed food similarly guarded from impurity and produced in accord with Levitical revelation. By contrast, the rabbi was like God because he studied the Torah on earth, as did God and Moses, "our rabbi" in the heavenly academy.

IV

Of the important sects known to us in the period before 70, present at Yavneh were surely the Pharisees and probably also a fair sampling of another sort of group, not a sect but a profession, namely, the scribes. It is, as I said, in the amalgamation of the method of pharisaism and the doctrine of scribism that Rabbinic

Judaism, with its stress on universal learning in Torah, emerges. We have a good picture of the viewpoint of a putative adherent, after 70, of the conceptions of pharisaism in the person of Eliezer b. Hyrcanus, an important authority of Yavneh. I may briefly summarize his conception of the laws necessary for the new age. Eliezer's legislation suggests he presumed life would soon go on pretty much as it had in the past. Issues important to pre-70 Pharisees predominate in his laws. Issues absent in the rabbinic traditions about the Pharisees are mostly absent in his as well. Eliezer therefore comes at the end of the old pharisaism. He does not inaugurate the new rabbinism, traces of which are quite absent in his historically usable traditions. Indeed, on the basis of his laws and sayings, we can hardly define what this rabbinism might consist of. The doctrine of the oral Torah, the view of the rabbi as the new priest and of study of Torah as the new cult, the definition of piety as the imitation of Moses "our rabbi" and the conception of God as a rabbi, the organization of the Jewish community under rabbinic rule and by rabbinic law, and the goal of turning all Israel into a vast academy for the study of the Torah— none of these motifs characteristic of later rabbinism occurs at all.

Since by the end of the Yavnean period the main outlines of rabbinism were clear, we may postulate that the transition from pharisaism to rabbinism, or the union of the two, took place in the time of Eliezer himself. But he does not seem to have been among those who generated the new viewpoints; he appears as a reformer of the old ones. His solution to the problem of the cessation of the cult was not to replace the old piety with a new one but, rather, to preserve and refine the rules governing the old in the certain expectation of its restoration in a better form than ever. Others, who were his contemporaries and successors, developed the rabbinic idea of the (interim) substitution of study for sacrifice, the rabbi for the priest, and the oral Torah of Moses "our rabbi" for the piety of the old cult.

V

Let us now turn to the scribes and their ideal of Torah. The scribes before 70 form a distinct group—not merely a profession— in the Gospels' accounts of Jesus' opposition. Scribes and Pharisees are by no means regarded as one and the same group. To be sure, what scribes say and do not say is not made clear. One cannot derive from the synoptic record a clear picture of scribal doctrine or symbolism, if any, although one certainly finds an account of the pharisaic law on ritual uncleanness and tithing. Since the materials now found in the synoptics were available in Palestine between 70 and 90, however, they may be presumed accurately to portray the situation of that time, because their picture had to be credible to Christians of the period. Now, having seen in Eliezer an important representative of the old pharisaism, we find no difficulty in accounting for the pharisaic component of the Yavnean synthesis. It likewise seems reasonable to locate in the scribes the antecedents of the ideological and symbolic part of the rabbinic component at Yavneh. Admittedly, our information on scribism in the rabbinic literature is indistinguishable from the later sayings produced by rabbinism. But if we consider that scribism goes back to much more ancient times than does pharisaism, and that its main outlines are clearly represented, for instance, by Ben Sira, we may reasonably suppose that what the scribe regarded as the center of piety was study, interpretation, and application of the Torah. To be sure, what was studied and how it was interpreted are not to be identified with the literature and interpretation of later rabbinism. But the scribal piety and the rabbinic piety are expressed through an identical symbol, study of Torah. And one looks in vain in the rabbinic traditions about the Pharisees before 70 for stress on, or even the presence of the ideal of, the study of Torah. Unless the Torah ideal of rabbinism begins as the innovation of the early Yavneans—and this seems to me unlikely—it therefore should represent at Yavneh the continuation of pre-70 scribism.

But pre-70 scribism continued with an important difference, for Yavnean and later rabbinism said what cannot be located in pre-70 scribal documents: The Temple cult is to be replaced by study of Torah, the priest by the rabbi (= scribe); and the center of piety was shifted away from cult and sacrifice entirely. So Yavnean scribism made important changes in pre-70 scribal ideas. It responded to the new situation in a more appropriate way than did the Yavnean Pharisaism represented by Eliezer. Eliezer could conceive of no piety outside of that focused upon the Temple. But Yavnean and later scribism-rabbinism was able to construct an expression of piety which did not depend upon the Temple at all. While Eliezer appears as a reformer of old pharisaism, the proponents of rabbinism do not seem to have reformed the old scribism. What they did was to carry the scribal ideal to its logical conclusion.

If study of Torah was central and knowledge of Torah important, then the scribe had authority even in respect to the Temple and the cult; indeed, his knowledge was more important than what the priest knew. This view, known in the sayings of Yohanan b. Zakkai, who certainly held that the priest in Yavnean times was subordinate to the rabbi, is not a matter only of theoretical consequence. Yohanan also held that he might dispose of Temple practices and take them over for the Yavnean center—and for other places as well—and so both preserve them ("as a memorial") and remove from the Temple and the priests a monopoly over the sacred calendar, festivals, and rites. Earlier scribism thus contained within itself the potentiality to supersede the cult. It did not do so earlier because it had no reason to and because it probably could not. The later rabbinism, faced with the occasion and the necessity, realized that potentiality. By contrast, earlier pharisaism invested its best energies in the replication of the cult, not in its replacement. After 70, it could do no more than plan for its restoration.

VI

Scribism as an ideology, not merely a profession, begins with the view that the law given by God to Moses was binding and therefore has to be authoritatively interpreted and applied to daily affairs. That view goes back to the fourth century B.C., by which time Nehemiah's establishment of the Torah of Moses as the constitution of Judea produced important effects in ordinary life. From that time on, those who could apply the completed, written Torah constituted an important class or profession. The writings of scribes stress the identification of Torah with wisdom and the importance of learning. Ben Sira's sage travels widely in search of wisdom and consorts with men of power. Into the first century, the scribes continue as an identifiable estate high in the country's administration. Otherwise, the synoptics' view is incomprehensible. Therefore, those who were professionally acquainted with the scriptures—whether they were priests or not—formed an independent class of biblical teachers, lawyers, administrators, or scribes alongside the priesthood. We do not know what they actually did in the administration of the country. Perhaps Yohanan b. Zakkai's reference to decrees of Jerusalem authorities (M. Ketubot 13:1ff.) alludes to the work of scribes, who therefore were involved—as the Pharisees certainly were not—in the determination of family law and in the settlement of trivial disputes.

The New Testament references support the supposition that the scribes were a separate group, differentiated from Sadducees and Pharisees. The scribes occur in association with the high priests in Matthew 2:4, 16:21, 20:18, 21:15, 27, 27:41; Mark 8:31, 10:33, 11:18, 27, 14:1, 43, 53, 15:1, 31, etc., with the Pharisees in Matthew 5:20, 12:38, 15:1, 23:2, 13 ff.; Mark 2:16, 7:1, 5. But they are not the same as the one or the other. The scribes are called "learned in the law" and jurists. (Matthew 22:35; Luke 7:30, 10:25, 11:45, 52, 14:3.) They are teachers of the law. (Luke 5:17; Acts 5:34.)

Mishnaic literature obviously will miss the distinction between Pharisees and scribes, both of whom are regarded as HKMYM, sages. But we have no reason to suppose all scribes were Pharisees. Scribes were merely "men learned in the law." There must have been also Sadducean scribes. In fact, those passages of the New Testament, which speak of scribes who were of the Pharisees (Mark 2:16, Luke 5:30, Acts 23:9) point also to the existence of Sadducean scribes (Schürer). The scribes therefore represent a class of men learned in scripture, perhaps lawyers in charge of the administration of justice. They therefore had to develop legal theories, teach pupils, and apply the law. Naturally, such people would come to the center of the administration of government and law, so they could not have remained aloof from Yavneh. Some of them may, to be sure, have come because they were Pharisees. But others, whatever their original ritual practices, would have come because Yavneh represented the place in which they might carry on their profession.

Josephus—himself a new adherent of the Pharisees—does not confuse the scribes with the Pharisees. In none of his allusions to the Pharisees does he also refer to the scribes (*grammateis*) or call Pharisees scribes. In *Life* 197-98, he refers to a delegation of Jerusalemites to Galilee. Two were from the lower ranks of society and adherents of the Pharisees, the third was also a Pharisee, but a priest; the fourth was descended from high priests. These were all able to assert that they were not ignorant of the customs of the fathers. To be sure, the Pharisees are referred to as knowledgeable in the Torah; and they have "traditions from the fathers" in addition to those that Moses had revealed. But they are not called scribes. They were (*War* 1:107-14) exact exponents of the laws. But again they are not called scribes. The long "philosophical school" account in *Antiquities* 18:11-17 describes the Pharisees as virtuous and says that "all prayers and sacred rites of divine worship are performed according to their exposition"—but they too are not scribes.

When Josephus does refer to scribes, he does not refer to Pharisees. For example, in *War* 1:648ff. (= *Antiquities* 17:152), he refers to two *sophistai* who ordered their disciples to pull down the eagle that Herod had set up in the Temple. They are Judah son of Sepphoraeus and Matthias son of Margalus, men who gave lectures on the laws, attended by a large, youthful audience. If these are scribes, they are not said also to be Pharisees, who do not occur in the account. We find also *hierogrammateis* and *patrion exegetai nomon*—but *not* in the context of the passages about the Pharisees. While, therefore, the Pharisees and the scribes have in common knowledge of the country's laws, the two are treated separately. Josephus does not regard the scribes as wholly within the pharisaic group; he presents the scribe as a kind of authority or professional teacher of law. Josephus does not associate scribes with Pharisees; no scribe is a Pharisee; and no Pharisee is described as a scribe. The two are separate and distinct. One is a sect, the other is a profession.

Since later rabbinism found pre-70 scribism highly congenial to its ideal, it is by no means farfetched to trace the beginnings of Yavnean rabbinism to the presence of representatives of the pre-70 scribal class, to whom the ideal of study of Torah, rather than the piety of the cult and the replication of that cultic piety in one's own home, was central. At Yavneh, therefore, were incorporated these two important strands of pre-70 times—the one the piety of a sect, the other the professional ideal of a class.

VII

To summarize: The Pharisees before 70 extended the Temple's sanctity to the affairs of ordinary folk, requiring that people eat their meals in a state of purity appropriate for the sanctuary and preserve their food from impurity originally pertinent only to the cult and priesthood. After 70 the rabbinical successors of pharisaism treated sacrifice itself as something to be done in everyday life, comparing deeds of loving-kindness to the sacrifices by which sins were atoned for. So it was an established trait of pharisaism and later rabbinism to apply cultic symbols to extra-cultic, communal matters, thus to regard the Temple's sanctity as extending to the streets of the villages. This was done after 70 by assigning ethical equivalents to Temple rites, on the one side, and by comparing study of Torah to the act of sacrifice and the rabbi to the Temple priest, on the other. Cultic purity was extended to the home, and, later on, study of Torah was substituted for cultic sacrifice and deeds of loving-kindness for sin-offering. Later it would be natural to take over the purity-rules and to endow them with ethical, therefore with everyday, communal significance, instead of leaving them wholly within the cult. It was a continuation of an earlier tendency to ethicize, spiritualize, and moralize the cult by treating the holy people—the community of Israel—as equivalent to the holy sanctuary. The rabbis' larger tendency thus is to preserve, but to take over within the rabbinical system, the symbols of the Temple. The rabbi is the new priest. Study of Torah is the new cult. Deeds of loving-kindness are the new sacrifice.

4

The Mishnah
As a Focus of
Torah-Piety

Now that we have considered the theological and historical aspects of the ideal of learning in Judaism, we come finally to the literary aspect. The conception of the centrality of Torah-learning is joined, by the end of the second century, to the notion that, at Sinai, Moses received a dual Torah, one in writing, the other handed on through oral formulation and oral transmission. That other half of divine revelation is constituted by Mishnah, a corpus of laws redacted at ca. A.D. 200. Along with scriptures, Mishnah is one of the two principal documents of that form of Judaism which has been predominant and normative since the third century, that Rabbinic Judaism of which I spoke at such length in the third lecture. Rabbinic Judaism stands upon the claim that two Torahs, together revealed at Sinai, constitute the one whole Torah of Moses, "our rabbi." Mishnah is transmitted, it is claimed, through processes of memorization and therefore is called "the Oral Torah," while the Pentateuch is the written one. Accordingly, when we come to Mishnah, we approach one of the principal foci of Torah-learning.

The question before us is this: What is the religious world-view expressed by the principal document of Rabbinic Judaism? How is piety expressed in a system in which Torah-learning is at the center? The first thing we have to know is that, to the formative minds of Rabbinic Judaism, praying is not the chief expression of piety and not the highest mode of liturgy. There is work for God which is to be done—that is, liturgy—and it is not chiefly in praying but in learning that that work is carried out. The view of the third- and fourth-century rabbis is representative: Praying concerns temporal needs. Learning is life eternal. So, for example, when Raba saw Hamnuna praying too long, he criticized him: "You forsake eternal life and occupy yourself with worldly needs" (Babylonian Talmud Shabbat 10a). Sheshet would turn aside and repeat Mishnah-traditions between the segments of the scriptural lection, saying, "They with theirs, and we with ours." (Ibid., Berakhot 8a.) When Isaac asked Nahman why he did not come to the synagogue in order to pray, Nahman replied, "I can't do so." "Why," Isaac asked, "does R. Nahman not gather ten people to pray with a quorum at home?" "Because," he said, "it is too much trouble." (Ibid., 7b.) Accordingly, so far as the cited rabbis are concerned, the synagogue as a place of praying is not a principal locus of the holy life. Eternal life is sought elsewhere.

We know from Lecture One that to the rabbis of Rabbinic Judaism in its formative centuries, man seeks transcendence through *Talmud Torah*, learning in divine revelation as handed on by the rabbis. Worship as liturgy, that is, work for God, is carried on not principally through praying, which is for our selfish needs, but through study. True worship takes its own intellectual forms. This fact requires us to revise our definition of worship, which usually deems worship equivalent to praying. We therefore ask, What is the meaning of the transcendence attained through learning? We turn, in particular, to the analysis of the religious world view of Rabbinic Judaism as revealed in the first, and generative, document of that form of Judaism, which is Mishnah. We treat the question in four parts: the rabbinic understanding of transcendence, forms of worship, modes of community, and uses of tradition.

Transcendence is the quest for something beyond oneself, the effort to surpass one's own being and to find what, in the supernatural world, it is that, in this world, we stand for: the effort to reach outward toward, and inward into, that image in which we are made. To the rabbis of the first seven centuries of the Common Era and to their continuators down to the contemporary expressions of Rabbinic Judaism, transcendence is to be attained in and through Torah. By Torah are meant a *book,* on the one side, and an *activity*—the act of learning—on the other. The "book" of course is the written scriptures, the Tanakh, and the unwritten revelation of God to Moses "our rabbi" at Mount Sinai. Thus *Torah* refers to "the whole Torah of Moses our rabbi," a Torah in two parts, distinguished by the forms of the formulation and transmission. The one part is written down. The other part is memorized. The two together constitute *Torah*, and what is done with the two is to learn Torah, principally through memorization and critical inquiry into what is memorized (that is, the paramount mode of the *second* half of Torah). Accordingly, literary texts constitute the utensils of the transcendent, and learning in them defines the quest for, and experience of, transcendence. It follows that, to the ancient rabbis and their continuators, one seeks God through the worship effected in a particular kind of learning of a distinctive sort of literature. The common sense of worship—praying—is, as I have emphasized, secondary and unimportant, an essentially worldly and non-transcendent activity.

To the rabbis Torah remains open, an uncompleted canon, as late as the early third century, and beyond. Mishnah, after all, is called Torah by people who know personally authorities of the Mishnah, e.g., by Samuel and Rab, who can have known Rabbi himself. No wonder, then, that they could deem Torah-learning to be the chief locus of the open way toward transcendence, for it is through the processes of *qabbalah* and *massoret*—handing down, traditioning—that they claim in behalf of Mishnah its status as part of Mosaic revelation: *Torah-learning is a mode of attaining revelation of Moses at Sinai,* and transcendence by rabbis is defined as receiving divine revelation. Mishnah itself is called Mosaic and assigned to Sinai by people who stand within decades of the furious redactional and tradental work which brought Mishnah into being, an amazing fact. Accordingly, so far as the talmudic rabbis are concerned, Torah is, as I said, an unfilled basket, a canon still (and, I think, perpetually) open and uncompleted. If Judah, Meir, Simeon, Yosé, and Simeon ben Gamaliel are the main authorities of Mishnah, moreover, it means that the third- and fourth-century rabbis cannot have supposed the processes of revelation had closed a thousand or more years earlier. Not for them the route of pseudepigraphy, assigning their great ideas to Adam or Enoch or the sons of Jacob. Nor do they even take the trouble to anachronize the language of the oral Torah and to put it into the forms and syntax of the biblical tongue, as do the masters of the Essene community at Qumran. They do not imitate the forms of the sacred literature of old nor hide themselves in the cloak of pseudepigraphic anonymity. For to them transcendence is as available now as it had been to Moses. And nothing said to Moses is not also said to them.

To the rabbis of talmudic times, therefore, the way to surpass themselves and to reach out to the godly way, the path to the imitation of Moses "our rabbi" and to the heavenly academy at which God studies Torah, lies in the very immediate present. It is now important to spell out the concrete modes of following or expressing the transcendental way characteristic of Torah-learning. For we now know that these constitute not solely salvific, but revelatory forms. Through the *way* in which rabbis learn Torah they know God, or, to be more precise, that part of God which was to be known by man: God's will and mind.

II

The modes under discussion pertain to method. First, how is Torah in the memorized form to be formulated and handed on? Second, how is Torah to be learned, that is, attained? The answer to the first question is that the part of Torah represented by Mishnah is so formulated as to be memorized. The answer to the second is that Torah is attained through the exegesis of Torah already attained. The open canon allows for the inclusion of new works of Torah into late medieval times, e.g., Zohar, Maimonides' *Mishneh Torah,* Joseph Karo's *Shulhan 'Arukh.* That is, the corpus of books holy to Rabbinic Judaism included not only the medieval compilations of midrash but also later works of law and mysticism. This, of course, poses a paradox, to which we shall have to return.

Let us dwell upon the matter of memorization. Mishnah is a work formulated in the processes of redaction. That is, the particular linguistic formulation of Mishnah takes place among the men who at the same time propose to put together the corpus of linguistic formulations into a well-composed and orderly document. They work with materials of the antecedent two or three centuries, but whatever forms were imposed on these materials in earlier times are wholly obliterated by men wholly in command of themselves and confident of their own superior judgment of how things should be put together and worded.

Mishnah is set out in highly stereotyped sentences, and the range of such sentences is very limited. We can list the paramount forms of Mishnaic language on the fingers of one hand. The patterned sentences, e.g., *If X is so, then Y is the rule, and if X is not so, then Y is not the rule,* will run on in groups of threes or fives. When the pattern shifts to some other, so too does the topic under discussion change. The patterns, moreover, are so worked out and put together that it is exceedingly easy to memorize Mishnah. Accordingly, just as the authorities of Mishnah do not take the trouble to put their ideas into the mouths of Adam, Enoch, or e.g., their own heroes, Moses and David, and just as they do not bother to copy the formulary patterns of scripture, so they take stunningly decisive action to wipe out the traces of the literary and aesthetic forms in which intellectual materials then nearly three centuries old had come down into their own hands. In this regard we are reminded of the work of aesthetic innovators in the great ages of architecture, who not only declined to imitate the buildings they saw around them, but tore down those buildings and made their own instead.

And, it is to be stressed, what the redactors and formulators of Mishnah do, they do only in Mishnah. The companion compilation, Tosefta, does not reveal any equivalent traits of formulation aimed at facilitating memorization. Nor in the later rabbinic documents do we find equivalent traits encompassing whole chapters and even larger units of redaction, though, to be sure, brief formularies seem to have been memorized throughout. It follows that Mishnah is something special and, I claim, unique. It alone is made into literature for memorization, and in its behalf alone is the claim laid down, "Moses received Torah at Sinai, and handed it on to Joshua, and Joshua to the sages, and sages to the prophets," and so on down to the named authorities who stand within the pages of Mishnah itself, even such recent figures as Shammai and Hillel, for example.

III

Exactly how do the framers of Mishnah facilitate memorization? Let me state first what they do not do. They do not give us rhyme schemes. While the document probably was meant to be sung, it does not follow disciplined rhythms. The principal forms of the Mishnaic sentence consist of consistent arrangements of words in certain syntactical patterns, not in the repetition of the same words with some stunning variation at the start or end of a thought. Accordingly, what makes it easy to memorize Mishnah is the presence of recurrent syntactical patterns. These are embedded deep within the structure of language, rather than expressed superficially, e.g., in concrete repetition of particular words, rhythms, syllabic counts, or sounds. The Mishnaic mnemonic is defined by the inner logic of word patterns: grammar and syntax. Even though Mishnah is to be memorized and handed on orally and not in writing, it expresses a mode of thought attuned to highly abstract syntactical relationships, not concrete and material ones. Rabbis who memorize Mishnah are capable of amazingly abstract perceptions.

For their ears and minds perceive regularities of grammatical arrangements among diverse words. What is memorized is a recurrent notion expressed in diverse examples but, as I said, framed in a single, repeated rhetorical pattern. Truth lies beneath the surface of diverse rules. It is the unstated principle which unites the stated cases, embedded in the deep structure of language and thought alike. (See above, pp. 6ff.)

Mishnaic rhetoric creates a world of discourse distinct from the concrete realities of a given time, place, and society. The exceedingly limited repertoire of grammatical patterns in which all ideas on all matters are expressed gives symbolic expression to the notion that beneath the accidents of life are comprehensive, unchanging, and enduring relationships. These patterns lie deep in the inner structure of reality and impose structure and meaning upon the accidents of the world.

It therefore is through *how* things are said, as much as through *what* is said, that Mishnah proposes to express its transcendent message. What is remarkable is that Mishnah expects to be understood. It is not gibberish, composed of meaningless rhymes or repeated words, repetition of which brings salvation. Mishnah is made out of meaningful statements, the *form* of which is meant to convey deep meaning. The framers of Mishnah, as I said, expect to be understood by keen ears and active minds. They therefore convey what is fundamental at the level of grammar, autonomous of specific meanings of words and cases. Thereby they manifest confidence that the listener will put many things together and draw the important conclusions for himself. Mishnah assumes an active intellect capable of perceiving implications and of vivid participation. Mishnah demands memorizing the message, but also perceiving the unarticulated message contained within the medium of syntax and grammar. And the hearer is assumed to be capable of putting the two together into still further insight. The cogent syntactical pattern underlying statements about different things expresses a substantive cogency among those diverse and divergent cases.

Mishnah claims to make wise and true statements, which, moreover, apply at any time and in any place. It follows that Mishnah proposes to describe how things truly are. And the people who make Mishnah do so in order to put together, in a single document and in encapsulated form, an account of the inner structure of reality. This account is, specifically, of that aspect of reality which, in their judgment, can and should be put into formally patterned words. All of the diverse and changing phenomena of the world can be reduced to a few simple, descriptive equations. These, I repeat, are expressed in particular by deep traits of the interrelationships of words, persistent patterns of grammar and syntax.

There are then these two striking traits of mind reflected within Mishnah: first, the perception of order and balance, and, second, the view of the mind's centrality in the construction of order and balance. The mind imposes wholeness upon discrete cases. Mind perceives meaning and pattern, because, to begin with, it is mind, the will, understanding, and intention of man, which *imparts* meaning to the world. To give one concrete example of that fact, I point out that, to the rabbis of the second century, it is human intention, not material reality or automatic working of mindless laws, which defines what is unclean or clean. In one area of the law of purities after another, the conclusion is reached that what man *thinks* is determinative of what can be made unclean and definitive of the processes of contamination. For instance, scripture states (Leviticus 11:34, 37) that if a dead creeping thing falls on food, and if the food is dry, it is unaffected, but if it is wet, it is made unclean. The late first- and second-century rabbis add, however, that food which is wet down accidentally is not affected by the source of uncleanness. It is still clean and insusceptible. Only when a man deliberately draws water and intentionally applies it to grain, for example, does the grain become susceptible to uncleanness. It follows that, if you have two stacks of grain, one on which rain has fallen, another which a man has watered, and if a dead creeping thing falls on both, only the latter is unclean. The two sorts of grain are identical, except for man's intention. This is one among literally hundreds of examples of the same viewpoint. My sense is that all the oral Torah wishes to say as its perspective of transcendence may be summed up in one verse: *"What is man, that thou art mindful of him, and the son of man, that thou thinkest of him? Yet thou has crowned him with glory and honor and made him little lower than the angels."*

IV

Mishnah comes into being in the aftermath of the Bar Kokhba War. That fact is heavy with meaning. For it is only after Bar Kokhba that ancient Israel knows beyond doubt the cult of the Temple in Jerusalem would not soon be restored. From 70 for three generations the hope was that, as 586 had been followed in three generations by Cyrus and the return to Zion, so 70 would be followed through divine intervention and the coming of a messiah. But with the end of the terrible war, it was forbidden for Jews to enter Jerusalem. Could anyone still have expected permission to rebuild the Temple and reestablish the cult? The second half of the second century, in which Mishnah takes over the teachings of scribes and Pharisees before 70 and rabbis afterward and makes of those teachings a principal component of the Torah of Moses, is the time of the reconsideration of the meaning of worship.

Clearly, worship through prayer was already ancient for the second-century Israelites. But worship through sacrifice also was an old and established mode of divine service. The loss of that second mode of worship cannot have been ignored. To state matters briefly: learning in Mishnah succeeds sacrifice in the cult as a mode of worship, and, I think, the succession is not temporal only, but bears deep ontological meaning. To explain this point, I cite the statement, in a lecture at Brown University, of William Scott Green, University of Rochester:

> If the performance of rituals within the Temple exposes the lines of God's revealed reality, then thinking ... about these rituals outside the Temple, even without the possibility of performing all of them, has the same result. The Mishnaic rabbis express their primary cognitive statements, their judgments upon large matters, through ... law, not through myth or theology, neither of which is articulated at all. Early Rabbinism took ritual beyond the realm of practice and transformed it into the object of speculation and the substance of thought. Study, learning, and exposition became ... the basic Rabbinic activity. ...

Restating this view in terms of Mishnaic grammatical rhetoric, we may say that the thinking about matters of detail within a particular pattern of cognitive constructions treats speculation and thought as themselves capable of informing and shaping being, not merely expressing its external traits: *Language becomes ontology.*

Language in Mishnah replaces cult. Formalism of one kind takes the place of formalism of another. The claim that infinitely careful and patterned doing of a particular sort of deeds is *ex opere operato* an expression of the sacred has its counterpart in the implicit character of Mishnah's language. Its rhetoric is formed with infinite care, according to a finite pattern for speech, about doing deeds of a particular sort. Language *now* conforms to cult *then.*

The formal cult, once performed in perfect silence, now is given its counterpart in formal speech. Where once men said nothing, but through gesture and movement, in other circumstances quite secular, performed holy deed, so now they do nothing. But through equally patterned revision of secular words about secular things, they perform holy speech. In the cult it is the very context which makes an intrinsically neutral, therefore secular, act into a holy one. Doing the thing right, with precision and studied care, makes the doing holy. Slaughtering an animal, collecting its blood, butchering it, burning incense, and pouring wine—these by themselves are things which can be, and are, done in the home as much as in the cult. But in the cult they are characterized by formality and precision.

In Mishnah, by contrast, there is no spatial context to sanctify the secular act of saying things. The context left, once cult is gone, is solely the cultic mode of formalism, the ritualization of speech, that most neutral and commonplace action. Mishnah transforms speech into ritual and so creates the surrogate of ritual deed. That which was not present in cult, speech, is all that is present now that the silent cult is gone. And, it follows, it is by the formalization of speech, its limitation to a few patterns, and its perfection through the creation of patterns of relationships in particular, that the old nexus of heaven and earth, the cult, now is to be replicated in the new and complementary nexus: cultic speech about all things.

V

How does the Mishnaic mode of liturgy—worship through learning—affect the life of the community? It brings to the center the importance of memorizing and carrying into everyday life the teachings of Torah. That is to say, in a world such as Mishnah's, in which writing is routine, memorization is special. What happens when we know something by heart which does not happen when we must read it or look for it in a scroll or a book is this: When we walk in the street and when we sit at home, when we sleep and when we awake, we carry with us, in our everyday perceptions, that memorized saying. The process of formulation through formalization and the co-equal process of memorizing patterned cases to sustain the perception of the underlying principle, uniting the cases just as the pattern unites their language, extends the limits of language to the outer boundaries of experience, the accidents of everyday life itself.

To impose upon those sayings an underlying and single structure of grammar corresponding to the inner structure of reality is to transform the structure of language into a statement of ontology. Once our minds are trained to perceive principle among cases and patterns within grammatical relationships, we further discern, in the concrete events of daily life, both principle and underlying autonomous pattern. The form of Mishnah is meant to correspond to the formalization perceived within, not merely imposed upon, the conduct of concrete affairs. The matter obviously is not solely ethical, though the ethical component is self-evident. It also has to do with the natural world and the things which break its routine. In Mishnah all things are a matter of relationship, circumstance, fixed and recurrent interplay. *If X, then Y, if not X, then not Y*—that is the datum by which minds are shaped.

The way to shape and educate minds is to impart into the ear, thence into the mind, perpetual awareness that what happens recurs, and what recurs is pattern and order, and, through them, wholeness. How better than to fill the mind with formalized sentences, generative of meaning for themselves and of significance beyond themselves? In such sentences meaning rests upon the perception of *relationship*. Pattern is to be discovered in alertness, in the multiplicity of events and happenings, none of which states or articulates pattern: Mind, trained to memorize through what is implicit and beneath the surface, is to be accustomed and taught in such a way to discern pattern. Order is because order is discovered, first in language, then in life. As the cult, in all its precise and obsessive attention to fixed detail, effected the perception that from the orderly center flowed lines of meaning to the periphery, so the very language of Mishnah, in its precise and obsessive concentration on innate and fixed relationship, effects the perception of order deep within the disorderly world of language, nature, and man.

VI

In my view, we misrepresent the rabbinic mode of transcendence when we call it "traditional." It is, I have argued, anything but tradition, in the commonplace sense of tradition as something handed on from of old which bears authority over us because it has been handed on from of old. The foundation of Mishnah's world view is the claim that revelation happens in Mishnah, which is the work of men of the recent past. Revelation continues to happen through learning in Mishnah.

It is the *contemporaneity* of Mishnah—a contemporaneity effected through the detachment of its cases from specific time and place and even particular linguistic context—which is its principal claim upon transcendence, that is, Mishnah's contemporaneity, not its status as "tradition." And the later history of Mishnah, its capacity to generate two large Talmuds as commentaries, its unfathomed implications stirring later generations to produce their commentaries to Mishnah and especially to its commentaries, their responses to specific questions of Torah-law, and their efforts to codify the law—these testify to the permanent contemporaneity of Mishnah down to the present day.

Accordingly, we must ask, Why is it that Mishnah, while Torah, prevents its own encapsulation and fossilization as tradition? In my view, the reason to begin with is to be found in the intentions of Mishnah's own framers, who do not present their ideas as ancient tradition but in their own names as living Torah, and who therefore keep open the path of continuing receptivity to transcendent truth through continuing use of mind. I think they do it deliberately, just as they intentionally reject the names of old authorities, the linguistic patterns of old documents, and the forms of worship established for more than a thousand years. In this context I cite the fine insight of S. C. Humphreys ("Transcendence and Intellectual Roles: The Ancient Greek Case," *Daedalus* 104, 1975, pp. 91-117; citation: pp. 112-113), who says:

> One of the factors influencing the intellectual to adopt a transcendental perspective appears to be the need to make his work comprehensible to an audience widely extended in space and continuing indefinitely into posterity. How far is our own appreciative response to these works—and especially to the rationalism of the Greek philosophers—due to the authors' deliberate intention of transcending limitations of social structure and temporal horizons? How far is this successful transcendence due to content and how far to form, to the structuring of the communication in such a way that it contains within itself enough information to make it immediately comprehensible? Is this a common quality of rational discourse and of "classic" works of art?

What I believe Miss Humphreys wishes to emphasize is that, when we respond to a document such as Mishnah and enter into its world, we do so because the people who make it as it is so framed it that we should do so.

Our response to the aesthetics of Mishnah—our recognition of how it is that matters are stated to facilitate memorization and, thereby, shape processes of cognition—is a tribute to the work of Rabbi and his colleagues. By stating Mishnah in terms essentially neutral to their own society (though, to be sure, drawing upon the data of their context), Rabbi sees to it that his part of the Torah will pass easily to other places and other ages. Through patterned language, Mishnah transcends the limitations of its own society and time. And, I have argued, a great part of this extraordinary creative achievement is in form, in the "structuring of the communication in such a way that it contains within itself enough information to make it immediately comprehensible."

And yet, there is a second side to matters. What makes Mishnah useful not only is its comprehensibility, but also *its incomprehensibility*. It is a deeply ambiguous document, full of problems of interpretation. Easy as it is to memorize, it is exceptionally difficult to understand. Mishnah not merely permits exegesis, it demands it. We can memorize a pericope of Mishnah in ten minutes. But it takes a lifetime to draw forth and understand the meaning. Mishnah contains within itself and, as I stress, even in its language, a powerful statement of the structure of reality. But that statement is so subtle that for eighteen hundred years, disciples of Mishnah, the Talmuds, and the consequent literature of exegesis, have worked on spelling out the meaning (not solely the concrete application) of that statement.

It is no accident at all that the most influential works of Jewish intellectual creativity, such as the Zohar and Maimonides' legal code, and that of Joseph Karo, link themselves specifically to Mishnah. Zohar claims for itself the same authorities as those of Mishnah, as if to say, "This is the other part of their Torah." And Maimonides' *Mishneh Torah*, as everyone knows, is in the model of, but an improvement upon, Mishnah itself. Nor should we forget that still a third religious genius of Judaism, Joseph Karo, heard the Mishnah speak to him and wrote down that the Mishnah had to say. These are diverse testimonies to the ineluctable demand, imposed by Mishnah itself for further exegesis. The one pseudepigraphic, the second an imitation of the language and form, and the third a curious personification of the document, all look backward, not forward.

For each is a way earlier taken in response to the written Torah. The Zohar takes the model—as to its authority—of the pseudepigrapha of the Old Testament. Maimonides, like the sages of the Essene community at Qumran, takes the model of the inherited linguistic choices of the holy book. Joseph Karo, of course, in his hearing the personification of Mishnah talking, will have been at home among those who talk of Torah or wisdom personified.

Among the greatest accomplishments of the history of Judaism, before or after its time, Mishnah stands all by itself in throwing aside all inherited models, even the logical potentialities of form and content explored before its own day and, as I just said, afterward as well. That, I think, is by far the most compelling evidence that Mishnah, for its part, is exactly what it claims to be: the work of revelation, fresh and surprising. It is Torah revealed to Moses at Sinai, therefore Torah not like the other half of Torah—*because it does not have to be.*

VII

Mishnah therefore is a fundamentally ahistorical document, because it does not appeal to the authority of the past. It does not represent itself as an exegesis of the ancient scripture. It generates a fundamentally ahistorical religion, that kind of Judaism predominant from its time to ours. Mishnah lays down timeless judgments and sets forth truths not subject to the judgment of history. Its preference for finding abstraction and order in concrete, perennial problems of daily life substitutes the criterion of reason and criticism for that of history and functionality. What counts is perennial reason. The object of reason is, first, the criticism of the given by the standard of fundamental principles of order, and second, the demonstration of the presence, within ordinary things, of transcendent considerations. The ultimate issue of Mishnah is how to discover the order of the well-ordered existence and well-correlated relationships. The prevalent attitude is perfect seriousness about man's intentions, therefore also about man's actions. The implicit goal of Mishnah is sanctification of the world through the use of the mind of men and women in the service of God. I therefore conclude where I began: The theory of Torah-piety expressed in the formative centuries of the Judaism which we know as normative is best stated very simply, "The glory of God is intelligence," to which, Judaism will add, "intelligence in perceiving revelation in creation, Torah in order and form, and the love and mercy of God even in our capacity to know."

Jacob Neusner

The lecturer is University Professor of Religious Studies, and The Ungerleider Distinguished Scholar of Judaic Studies at Brown University, Providence, Rhode Island. He holds the A.B., *Magna cum laude* in history, from Harvard College; the M.H.L. from The Jewish Theological Seminary of America; and the Ph.D. from Columbia University. He has held the Henry Fellowship at Oxford University and the Fulbright Scholarship at the Hebrew University, Jerusalem, as well as fellowships from the American Council of Learned Societies and the John Simon Guggenheim Memorial Foundation. Before going to Brown in 1968, he taught for four years at Dartmouth College. He holds the following academic affiliations, awards, and offices:

1960-   Life Member, American Oriental Society
1965-   Elected Member, American Society for the Study of Religion
1967-68   Vice President and Program Chairman, American Academy of Religion
1968-69   President, American Academy of Religion

1968-	Association for Jewish Studies, Member, Founding Committee; Member, Board of Directors, 1968-1972
1968-69	Council on the Study of Religion, Member, Founding Committee; Delegate, American Academy of Religion.
1968-	Fellow, Royal Asiatic Society (London)
1969	A.M. Ad Eundem, Brown University
1969-	President, The Max Richter Foundation
1972	Elected Fellow, American Academy for Jewish Research, 1976-, Member, Executive Committee
1973-	Editor, *Studies in Judaism in Late Antiquity* (Monograph Series, E. J. Brill, Leiden)
1974	University Medal for Excellence, Columbia University, Conferred May 15, 1974
1975-	Editor, *Studies in Judaism in Modern Times* (Monograph Series, E. J. Brill, Leiden)
1975-	Editor, *Library of Judaic Learning* (Textbook Series, Ktav Publishing House, New York)
1976-	Editorial Board, *The New Review of Books and Religion* (Seabury)
1976-	Editor, *Brown Judaic Studies* (Monograph Series, Scholars Press)
1977	Visiting Professor of Rabbinic Literature, Jewish Theological Seminary of America (Graduate School, Summer Session)

He has published the following scholarly books:

A Life of Yohanan ben Zakkai. Leiden: E. J. Brill, 1962. Awarded Abraham Berliner Prize in Jewish History, Jewish Theological Seminary of America, 1962. Second Edition, completely revised, 1970.

A History of the Jews in Babylonia. Leiden: E. J. Brill.

I.	*The Parthian Period* (1965). Second printing, revised, 1969.
II.	*The Early Sasanian Period* (1966).
III.	*From Shapur I to Shapur II* (1968).

IV.   *The Age of Shapur II* (1969).

V.   *Later Sasanian Times* (1970).

Development of a Legend: Studies on the Traditions Concerning Yohanan ben Zakkai. Leiden: E. J. Brill, 1970.

Aphrahat and Judaism: The Christian-Jewish Argument in Fourth Century Iran. Leiden: E. J. Brill, 1971.

The Rabbinic Traditions about the Pharisees before 70. Leiden: E. J. Brill, 1971.

I.   *The Masters.*

II.   *The Houses.*

III.   *Conclusions.*

Eliezer ben Hyrcanus: The Tradition and the Man. Leiden: E. J. Brill, 1973.

I.   *The Tradition.*

II.   *The Man.*

The Idea of Purity in Ancient Judaism. The 1972-73 Haskell Lectures. Leiden: E. J. Brill, 1973.

A History of Mishnaic Law of Purities. Leiden: E. J. Brill.

I.   *Kelim. Chapters One through Eleveen* (1974).

II.   *Kelim. Chapters Twelve through Thirty* (1974).

III.   *Kelim. Literary and Historical Problems* (1975).

IV.   *Ohalot. Commentary* (1975).

V.   *Ohalot. Literary and Historical Problems* (1974).

VI.   *Negaim. Mishnah-Tosefta* (1975).

VII.   *Negaim. Sifra* (1975).

VIII.   *Negaim. Literary and Historical Problems* (1975).

IX.   *Parah. Commentary* (1976)

X.   *Parah. Literary and Historical Problems* (1976).

XI.   *Tohorot. Commentary* (1976).

XII.   *Tohorot. Literary and Historical Problems* (1976).

XIII.   *Miqvaot. Commentary* (1976).

XIV.   *Miqvaot. Literary and Historical Problems* (1976).

XV.   *Niddah. Commentary* (1976).

XVI.   *Niddah. Literary and Historical Problems* (1976).

XVII.   *Makhshirin* (1977).

XVIII.   *Zabim* (1977).

XIX.   *Tebul Yom. Yadayim* (1977).

XX.   *Uqsin. Cumulative Index, Parts I-XX* (1977).

XXI. *The Redaction and Formulation of the Order of Purities in Mishnah and Tosefta* (1977).

XXII. *The Mishnaic System of Uncleanness: Its Context and History* (1977).

The Tosefta. Translated from the Hebrew. Sixth Division: Tohorot. New York: Ktav Publishing House, 1977.

The Tosefta. Translated from the Hebrew. Fifth Division: Qodoshim. New York: Ktav Publishing House, 1978.

A History of the Mishnaic Law of Holy Things. Leiden: E. J. Brill.

I. *Zebahim. Translation and Explanation* (1978).

II. *Menahot. Translation and Explanation* (1978).

III. *Hullin, Bekhorot. Translation and Explanation* (1978).

IV. *Arakhin, Temurah. Translation and Explanation* (1979).

V. *Keritot, Meilah, Tamid, Middot, Qinnim. Translation and Explanation* (1979).

VI. *The Mishnaic System of Holy Things: Its Context and History* (1979).

He has edited the following scholarly books:

Religions in Antiquity: Essays in Memory of Erwin Ramsdell Goodenough. Leiden: E. J. Brill, 1968: Supplements to Numen XIV.

Formation of the Babylonian Talmud: Studies in the Achievements of Late Nineteenth and Twentieth Century Historical and Literary-Critical Research. Leiden: E. J. Brill, 1970.

The Modern Study of the Mishnah. Leiden: E. J. Brill, 1973.

Soviet Views of Talmudic Judaism: Five Papers by Yu. A. Solodukho. Leiden: E. J. Brill, 1973.

Christianity, Judaism, and Other Greco-Roman Cults. Studies for Morton Smith at Sixty. Leiden: E. J. Brill, 1975.

I. *New Testament.*

II. *Early Christianity.*

III. *Judaism before 70.*

IV. *Judaism after 70. Other Greco-Roman Cults.*

He has written or edited the following textbooks:

The Way of Torah: An Introduction to Judaism. Encino: Dickenson

Publishing Company, 1970, in *Living Religions of Man* series, edited by Frederick Streng.

Editor: *The Life of Torah. Readings in the Jewish Religious Experience.* Encino: Dickenson Publishing Company, 1974, in *Living Religions of Man* series, edited by Frederick Streng.

There We Sat Down: Talmudic Judaism in the Making. Nashville: Abingdon Press, 1972. Second printing, New York: Ktav Publishing House, 1977.

American Judaism. Adventure in Modernity. Englewood Cliffs: Prentice-Hall, 1972.

From Politics to Piety: The Emergence of Pharisaic Judaism. Englewood Cliffs: Prentice-Hall, 1973.

Editor: *Contemporary Judaic Fellowship, in Theory and in Practice.* New York: Ktav Publishing House, 1972.

Invitation to the Talmud: A Teaching Book. New York: Harper & Row, 1973.

Editor: *Understanding Jewish Theology: Classical Themes and Modern Perspectives.* New York: Ktav Publishing House, 1973.

Editor: *Understanding Rabbinic Judaism. From Talmudic to Modern Times.* New York: Ktav Publishing House, 1974.

First-Century Judaism in Crisis. Yohanan ben Zakkai and the Renaissance of Torah. Nashville and New York: Abingdon Press, 1975.

Between Time and Eternity: The Essentials of Judaism. Encino: Dickenson Publishing Company, 1976.

Editor: *Understanding American Judaism. Toward the Description of a Modern Religion. I. The Synagogue and the Rabbi.* New York: Ktav Publishing House, 1975.

Editor: *Understanding American Judaism. Toward the Description of a Modern Religion. II. The Sectors of American Judaism: Reform, Orthodoxy, Conservatism, and Reconstructionism.* New York: Ktav Publishing House, 1975.

Let's Learn Mishnah. Let's Make Mishnah. New York: Behrman House, 1977 (Textbook for pre-teenagers).

He has, in addition, published the following collections of essays:

Fellowship in Judaism: The First Century and Today. London: Vallentine, Mitchell & Co., 1963.

61

History and Torah. Essays on Jewish Learning. London: Vallentine, Mitchell & Co., 1965; and New York: Schocken Books, 1965; paperback edition, New York: Schocken Books, 1967.

Judaism in the Secular Age. Essays on Fellowship, Community, and Freedom. London: Vallentine, Mitchell & Co., 1970; and New York: Ktav Publishing House, 1970.

Early Rabbinic Judaism. Historical Studies in Religion, Literature, and Art. Leiden: E. J. Brill, 1975.

The Academic Study of Judaism. Essays and Reflections. New York: Ktav Publishing House, 1975.

Talmudic Judaism in Sasanian Babylonia. Essays and Studies. Leiden: E. J. Brill, 1976.

The Academic Study of Judaism. Essays and Reflections. Second Series. New York: Ktav Publishing House, 1977.

General Index

Biblical and Talmudic Index